Medieval
Sovereignty

PAST IMPERFECT

See further
www.arc-humanities.org/our-series/pi

Medieval Sovereignty

Andrew Latham

British Library Cataloguing in Publication Data
A catalogue record for this book is available from the British Library

ISBN (print) 9781641892940
e-ISBN (PDF) 9781641892957
e-ISBN (EPUB) 9781641895002

www.arc-humanities.org
Printed and bound in the UK (by CPI Group [UK] Ltd), USA (by Bookmasters),
and elsewhere using print-on-demand technology.

Contents

Prologue 1

Chapter 1.   The Character of Supreme Authority:
             Quanto personam 15

Chapter 2.   The Locus of Supreme Authority:
             Per venerabilem 31

Chapter 3.   Conflict over Taxation 45

Chapter 4.   Conflict over Jurisdiction 55

Epilogue 93

Further Reading 97

To Wendy, Bernadette, and Michael
Omnia meae debeo familiae!

Prologue

The central problem for historians of the foundations of modern international thought should...be, "How did we"—whoever "we" may be—"come to imagine that we inhabit a world of states?"

David Armitage, *Foundations of Modern International Thought*[1]

Jean Bodin (1529/30–1596) exaggerated the novelty of his analysis of political power, and historians have exaggerated the novelty of his exaggeration. That Bodin stressed his originality is forgivable; that is an author's prerogative. That historians have accepted his contention without careful scrutiny is less understandable.

Kenneth Pennington, *The Prince and the Law, 1200–1600*

This book has two main aims. The first is to provide a tightly focused account of the most pivotal episode in the historical evolution of the idea of sovereignty—which I define generically as the supreme authority to command, legislate, and judge—in the thirteenth century. Although the existing historiographical literature is replete with studies that trace the evolution of that idea—even if they don't use the word "sovereignty" to describe it—in the fourteenth, fifteenth, and sixteenth centuries, no such account exists for the thirteenth century. To be certain, over the past half-century or

---

1 Works not referenced in the footnotes or only in short form there are fully cited in the Further Reading at the end of this work.

so a great deal of research has been done on aspects of the political thought during this era. But these efforts have tended to be fragmented, following different lines of inquiry, and emphasizing different themes. A conceptually focused interpretation, one foregrounding the role played by thirteenth century thought in the evolution of a coherent theory of sovereignty, has been lacking. My hope here is to begin to address this lacuna by providing an account of how a series of thirteenth-century contests over the locus and character of supreme authority ultimately made it possible "to imagine that we inhabit a world of [sovereign] states."

My secondary goal, hinted at in the epigraphs above, is to reconnect early modern theorists of sovereignty to the medieval intellectual tradition out of which they emerged. Thinkers like Bodin and Vattel did not invent the modern concept of sovereignty out of whole cloth. Rather, they assembled it out of the intellectual resources inherited from their medieval forebears, in the first instance from fourteenth-century thinkers like Marsilius, Baldus, and Bartolus, but via them from the thirteenth-century thinkers discussed in this book. While the specific questions they sought to address may have been unique to the early modern moment, and while there is no gainsaying the novelty and impact of their contributions, it is a central aim of this book to demonstrate that the early modern theorists of sovereignty were in a very real sense the apotheosis of a centuries-long medieval tradition of philosophical speculation about the locus and character of supreme authority.

This second claim, of course, contradicts the arguments, assertions, and assumptions of what I will call the "modernist" school of the history of the idea of sovereignty. Doubtless out of an abundance of concern with some scholars' claims regarding the transhistorical and immutable nature of "sovereignty," most modernists simply refute the very existence of a medieval sovereign state or the constitutive idea upon which such a state might be constructed. While the line of argumentation developed in these works is understandable, and at times quite illuminating of the non-statist aspects of medieval political life, it is also disappointing; for it means that the existing modernist literature practically erases the entire pre-history of the modern political order—and especially the pre-history of the early modern state-building project and the ideas driving, shaping, and conditioning that project.

Underpinning the specific weaknesses of this viewpoint is a tendency to unduly exoticize the medieval world, treating it as both mysterious and radically different from the modern one. Almost without exception, existing modernist accounts are premised on what Sverre Bagge has called the "Great Divide." On one side of that divide is the definitively modern idea of sovereignty and its derivative state and state-system, changing and evolving to be sure, but easily comprehensible to modernist scholars trained to think in terms of these categories. On the other side of the divide is the medieval world, an "orientalized" Other comprising an exotic congeries of ideas, institutions, and structures that are so alien as to render the epoch simultaneously both irrelevant to the study of modern political life and inaccessible to the contemporary modernist scholar.

Simply stated, modernists almost unanimously assert, assume, or argue that the medieval world order did not comprise states organized around the idea of sovereignty, but around a distinctively medieval organizing principle (feudalism and hierarchy being the usual suspects) that produced functionally differentiated polities (never states) subject to different laws of development. External sovereignty, they maintain, was impossible because of the universalist claims of the pope and emperor, both of whom claimed and exercised authority over kingdoms, principalities, and cities. Similarly, internal sovereignty was short-circuited by feudalism, custom, and ecclesiastical and temporal "liberties," all of which meant that there was no supreme locus of political authority within any given polity.

The result of all this, modernists maintain, was that Latin Christendom was segmented politically into several qualitatively distinct types of political unit—the Holy Roman Empire, the Catholic Church, city-states, urban leagues, feudal lordships, principalities, kingdoms, and even guilds and monasteries—all of which were structured around some combination of territorially non-exclusive and overlapping feudo-vassalic networks and pervasive papal and imperial hierarchical structures. By way of contrast, modernists typically argue, assert, or assume that the post-medieval or modern world order is made up of separate, territorially exclusive, functionally isomorphic states possessing both internal and external sovereignty.

This study rejects this perspective, arguing instead that sovereignty as a theologically inflected political concept decisively crystallized in the Latin Christian political imagination sometime around the turn of the fourteenth century. Specifically, the argument I will develop will unfold as follows. At the turn of the thirteenth century, two basic models of sovereignty were in circulation in Latin Christendom. On the one hand, there was the "hierocratic model." This model accepted that the *societas christiana* was divided into two domains or orders—spiritual and temporal—each governed by its own distinctive powers, but argued that as the spiritual power exceeded the temporal in honour and dignity, the spiritual exceeded the temporal in power and jurisdiction. According to this view, the spiritual power in effect mediated between God and the temporal powers, instituting the latter on God's behalf and judging it if it failed to do His will. Supreme authority was not shared by two coordinate powers but vested in the spiritual power alone. This power could delegate the material sword to the temporal authority, but that authority was then expected to wield it in the service of God and His Church. If it did not, the spiritual power could remove the material sword from the prince's hand and transfer it to someone more worthy.

On the other hand, there was the "dualist–imperialist model." On this view, the *societas christiana* was still divided into two domains or orders—lay and clerical—each of which had a distinctive way of life and governed by its own distinctive power. But, in an already well-established analogy drawn from scripture, emperors were said to wield the material sword and govern the temporal domain (the universal Empire), while popes wielded the spiritual sword and governed the spiritual domain (the universal Church). In this model, neither power infringed on the jurisdiction of the other. Both derived their powers directly from God, and while the spiritual power enjoyed greater dignity, this did not translate into greater power, authority, or jurisdiction. Supreme authority to legislate, command, and judge was thus divided between two coordinate powers: the Church and the Empire.

By the turn of the fourteenth century, however, these two models had decisively given way to a radically new one, which I will call the "dualist–regnalist" model.[2] According to this model, supreme authority was vested neither in the pope nor the emperor; nor was it divided between coordinate temporal and spiritual powers (kings and popes). Instead, it was vested exclusively in the king, who held it directly from God or (in the case of John of Paris, for example) "the people," without any papal or imperial mediation. Significantly, and in a radical break with the established norms of the preceding several centuries, this new political vision held that the king's supreme authority to legislate, command, and judge applied to the clergy as well as the laity, at least concerning temporal matters. Despite periodic nostalgic efforts to revive the hierocratic model (Alvarus Pelagius and Augustinus Triumphus) and the imperialist one (Englebert of Admont and Dante Alighieri), this new model would emerge triumphant by the middle decades of the fourteenth century (in the works of Marsilius of Padua, Baldus, Bartolus, and others).[3]

In this volume, I examine what is perhaps the key "inflection point" in this historical process, tracing how a bitter conflict between King Philip IV of France and Pope Boniface

---

2 Following Susan Reynolds, I use the word "regnal" to convey that the referent object of claims to sovereignty was the *regnum* or kingdom: Susan Reynolds, *Kingdoms and Communities in Western Europe 900–1300*, 2nd ed. (Oxford: Clarendon Press, 1997), 254.

3 Francis Oakley, *The Watershed of Modern Politics: Law, Virtue, Kingship, and Consent (1300–1650)*, (New Haven: Yale University Press, 2015).

VIII at the turn of the fourteenth century resulted in both the effective extinction of the hierocratic vision and the mutation of dualism into something qualitatively different from what it had been during the thirteenth century. My main argument is that in defending the right of the French king to try French clerics in French courts in the opening years of the fourteenth century, the pro-royal polemicists (represented by John of Paris) not only realized their goal of demolishing the hierocratic conceptual framework but in the process quite inadvertently undermined the premises of the dualist–imperialist one as well.[4] Drawing on the theological, juristic, and philosophical resources available to them—and especially the fruits of the papal decretals *Quanto personam* and *Per venerabilem*—they collectively developed a new political vision, characterized by novel and distinctive arguments and assumptions regarding the locus and character of supreme authority. While this process was not completed until the middle of the fourteenth century, and while its ultimate culmination did not occur until the sixteenth century, by the time of Boniface's death in 1303 it was certainly well underway.

In order to facilitate analysis of this episode of rapid conceptual mutation and innovation and bring into sharper relief whatever patterns of transformation might emerge, I have organized my treatment of it around two sets of organizing themes. The first of these has to do with the *character* of sovereignty—that is, with the historically specific way in which the meaning of supreme authority is articulated and delimited. Among the more important of these concepts are *legibus solutus* (loosed from the laws), *plenitudo potestatis* (fullness of power), *potesta absoluta* (absolute power), and *pro ratione voluntas* (by reason of will).

The second set of organizing questions has to do with the *locus* of sovereignty. Specifically, each chapter attempts to

---

4 In the first half of the fourteenth century, the idea of regnal sovereignty was further developed by thinkers such as Oldradus de Ponte, Marsilius of Padua, Bartolus of Saxoferrato, and Baldus de Ubaldis.

map how those engaged in political disputes thought about the location of supreme authority. Was sovereignty vested in the person of the emperor? The pope? The king? Or was it vested in more abstract or collective institutions such as the "crown," "the council," or even "the people"? Each chapter also seeks to illuminate the various ways in which canonists and polemicists justified and explained their respective conclusions regarding the proper locus of supreme authority.

With these questions in mind, Chapter 1 recounts how, in glossing the decretal *Quanto personam*, canon lawyers speculated on and ultimately defined the character of sovereignty—that is, how these jurists framed the distinctive and defining qualities of the supreme authority to command, legislate, and judge. Chapter 2 explores how the decretal *Per venerabilem* and its glosses specified the ultimate locus or site of that supreme authority. Taken together, these two chapters demonstrate that the ideas about the character and locus of supreme authority—ideas that would later at the turn of the fourteenth century be assembled into an increasingly coherent theory of sovereignty—were developed and refined in debates about canon law over the course of the thirteenth century. This is not to suggest, of course, that similar ideas were not evolving in the field of civil or Roman law. Given the interpenetration of the two domains of jurisprudence—collectively referred to as the *ius commune*—this would be highly unlikely indeed. And, indeed, in Chapter 2 I undertake a brief excursus into the realm of Roman law as it dealt with the crime of treason, primarily to demonstrate that such a parallel thread existed. Rather, it is merely to bracket out the civil law for heuristic purposes—that is, to focus more closely on the evolutionary dynamics taking place in the domain of canon law and its associated realms of political theology and polemics, and to focus specifically on those ideas actually taken up and used in the debate covered in the final two chapters of this volume.[5] This primary focus on canon law to the exclusion

---

5 For an overview of the civil law treatment of *imperium* and

of civil law is also recommended by the fact the historical personage whom I identify as the true progenitor of the "modern" idea of sovereignty, John of Paris, was a philosopher, theologian, and Dominican friar. He did not rely on, or communicate in the idiom of, Roman law.

The final half of the book examines the pivotal episode in this dynamic—the turn-of-the-fourteenth century dispute between King Philip IV of France and Pope Boniface VIII. It does this by tracing how protagonists in this political dispute over the locus and character of supreme authority drew on the language developed by the canon lawyers to develop an idea of sovereignty that would have been recognizable to Bodin and other early modern legists and political thinkers. In Chapter 3, I recount the first phase in this dispute in which Philip and Boniface contended over King Philip's right to tax members of the French clergy to help finance his war against England. Chapter 4 surveys the second phase of this dispute, which had to do with conflicting views on the topic of royal jurisdiction over French clerics.

Before proceeding to the substance of my argument, let me say a few words about methodology. This study adopts a modified "contextualist" approach, one that focuses on "ideas" rather than "texts," and I take a "diachronic" rather than "synchronic" perspective. It is contextualist in that it adopts the basic methodological approach of the Cambridge School.[6] Like the original proponents of this school—most famously Quentin Skinner, John Dunn, and J. G. A. Pocock—I reject the "unit-idea" approach of Lovejoy and his associates,

---

dominium during this era, see Daniel Lee, *Popular Sovereignty in Early Modern Constitutional Thought* (New York: Oxford University Press, 2016).

6 For an overview, see Mark Bevir, "The Contextual Approach," in *The Oxford Handbook of the History of Political Philosophy*, ed. George Klosko (Oxford, 2011), 11–23. Regarding the current state of the art, see Danielle Charette and Max Skjönsberg, "State of the Field: The History of Political Thought," *History: Journal of the Historical Association* 105, no. 366 (2020): 407–83.

with its focus on fixed ideas floating freely across time. Also like Skinner, and others, I oppose the Straussian search for hidden messages, the materialist reductionism of Marxists, and the post-structuralist skepticism regarding the possibility of an unmediated reading of the past. What I embrace in place of these modes of understanding the history of political thought is the core contextualist insight that political utterances and action must always be understood in its time, place, situation, and circumstances, never through tracing "decontextualised," essentialized unit-ideas down through the ages. Along with the contextualists, I assume that failure to do this leaves the door open to the twin perils of presentism and anachronism, both of which are always immanent in retrospective interpretations of history.

This study, then, is essentially contextualist in spirit: it takes as its point of departure the assumption that "sovereignty" is not a transhistorical concept passed down through the ages, shaping and reshaping political life in different ways as it touches down in differing historical contexts. Rather, it takes as its jumping off point the assumption that the idea of "sovereignty" (whatever word is used to capture and convey that idea) is always an historically specific answer to the recurring question, posed in different ways in different contexts, "what is the nature, source, and locus of supreme authority?"

But while I have embraced the foundational insights of the Cambridge School, I have of necessity modified them in two significant ways. First, following Mark Bevir's lead, I have adopted a focus on "ideas" instead of texts.[7] Bevir argues that historians of political thought should take ideas, rather than texts, as their object of analysis, and that they should treat texts as one medium (among many) for the expression

---

7 Mark Bevir, *The Logic of the History of Ideas* (Cambridge: Cambridge University Press, 1999). For a discussion of Bevir's work in this area see "Mark Bevir and the Logic of the History of Ideas," special isssue, *History of European Ideas* 28, no. 1–2 (2002): 1–100.

of ideas rather than as the sole object of historical interest. This is a significant reframing, for it transforms the history of ideas from a search for authors' bounded intentions when writing a particular text to a fuller exploration of the ideas that made the text possible in the first place—and which the text might, in turn, recursively refine, rework, or reconstruct. As Bevir puts it:

> ...the key task of the intellectual historian is the recovery, not of the illocutionary force of texts, but the relevant beliefs. Intellectual historians need not focus on what an author was doing in a text. They can focus on the complex interconnections among an author's beliefs and arguments. Alternatively, they can focus on narratives about intellectual movements and the shifting patterns of beliefs and commitments embedded therein.[8]

Focusing on ideas rather than texts, Bevir concludes, allows us to focus on the dynamics of change and innovation in the history of political thought, rather than simply on explaining the relationship of a text to political language, authorial intention, and historical circumstance.

Second, following the lead of David Armitage,[9] I have turned away from the synchronic bias of the Cambridge School. Like the contextualists, Armitage is interested in historicizing political thought. Unlike contextualists, however, Armitage employs a method that is diachronic rather than synchronic in nature—that is, one that focuses on tracing change across time rather than on developing snapshots of single, discrete moments. Since the contextualist revolution in the 1960s, most self-identified contextualists have treated context synchronically—that is, limited to discrete and tem-

---

8 Mark Bevir, "*The Logic of the History of Ideas* Then and Now," in "Post-Analytic Hermeneutics: Themes from Mark Bevir's Philosophy of History," special issue, *Intellectual History Review* 21, no. 1 (2011): 105–19, at 110.

9 David Armitage, "What's the Big Idea? Intellectual History and the *longue durée*," *History of European Ideas* 38, no. 4 (2012): 493–507.

porally limited episodes that are discontinuous with other episodes. Armitage, on the other hand, advocates something he calls "serial contextualism"—that is, the construction of a sequence of distinct contexts in which situated actors strategically deploy existing political concepts and arguments to advance or defend a particular point of view. Such a synthesis of *longue durée* historiography with the spirit of contextualism, he argues, allows for the reconstruction of "longer-range histories which are neither artificially punctuated nor deceptively continuous" (Armitage, 499).

With these modifications in place, it should be possible to trace the historical evolution of the history of the idea of sovereignty while avoiding both the Scylla of presentism and anachronism and the Charybdis of a radical historicism that would preclude any sort of diachronic study. In the abstract, my goal is to use this methodology to show how situated yet active historical agents—people engaged in concrete disputes (which may be political, theological, or even merely academic)—drew on the cultural and ideational resources available to them (typically transmitted via traditions and expressed in specific intellectual languages) to develop arguments that explain, advance, or defend their position. More concretely, my objective is twofold. First, to show how ideas related to power and authority circulating prior to the thirteenth century were, over the course of that century, hammered into the precursors of a theory of sovereignty against the anvil of two political-theological debates that unfolded over the course of that century—the debates over the papal bulls *Quanto personam* and *Per venerabilem*. And second, to show how John of Paris drew on the raw materials furnished by thinkers engaged in those earlier debates, as well as those used by his opponents in the Boniface–Phillip contest at the turn of the fourteenth century, to articulate the first coherent theory of regnal sovereignty in his work *De potestate regia et papali*.

Finally, a few words about the scope of this study. A complete account of the evolution of the idea of sovereignty, of course, would entail tracing the evolution of its character or constituent concepts (*iurisdictio*; *legibus solutus*; *plenitudo potestatis*; *potesta absoluta*; *pro ratione voluntas*; *persona ficta*; and *dominium*) across a number of distinct sites of political theorizing (canon law; Roman law; various polemical literatures; and the works of theologians and philosophers) over the course of several centuries. It would also entail tracing the evolution of the ultimately pervasive belief that the *locus* of supreme authority to command, legislate, and judge was properly vested in kingdoms and other principalities that recognized no superior across those same sites and over the same span of centuries. Finally, it would entail tracing the evolution of the idea that the *source* of supreme political authority some sort of synthesis of "the people" and God. In short, it would entail showing how the ideas that crystallized in the thirteenth century were subsequently received, reworked, and then relayed to the early modern "inventors" of sovereignty by fourteenth-century thinkers such as Marsilius of Padua (ca. 1275–ca. 1342), Bartolus de Saxoferrato (ca. 1313–1357), and Baldus de Ubaldis (1327-1400), and fifteenth-century thinkers such as Nicholas of Cusa (1401-1464) and John Fortescue (ca. 1394-1479)—all of whom were themselves engaged in their own historically specific debates over the character and locus of supreme political authority.[10] In this brief volume, however, my goal is somewhat less ambitious: to trace the evolution of several key concepts that became definitive of the character, locus, and source of supreme political authority during four distinct episodes of rapid conceptual evolution in the thirteenth century. The argument I develop is that, in the text and glosses of *Quanto personam* and *Per venerabilem* Pope Innocent III and the canonists made a number of important contributions to the idea of supreme authority—ideas that would subsequently be refined in the context of the dispute between Boniface and Philip, and that would ultimately cul-

---

10 See, for example, Joseph Canning, *Ideas of Power in the Late Middle Ages, 1296-1417* (Cambridge: Cambridge University Press, 2011).

minate in the work of John of Paris. I leave it to others to pick up the thread and weave it into a broader tapestry connecting those ideas developed in the thirteenth century to those that took shape both before and after that fateful century.

Chapter 1

The Character of Supreme Authority
Quanto personam

The political decretals issued by the popes during the thirteenth century profoundly re-shaped thinking about the
locus and character of supreme political authority.[1] On the
one hand, the popes themselves took canon law in new
directions, developing new justifications for papal power and
re-working older justifications in ways that amplified papal
authority over both bishops and temporal princes. On the
other hand, the canon lawyers struggled to bring greater
legal precision to the often-vague ideas introduced by the
popes. In this chapter, I trace one current in the evolution of
the language of supreme authority in canon law—that dealing with the character of supreme authority in the decretal
Quanto personam. I do this by examining how ideas introduced in this very influential papal decretal morphed and
mutated as a result of being glossed, either directly or indirectly, by influential canon lawyers, in the process providing
much of the raw material that the intellectual protagonists in
the conflict between Boniface and Philip would use to assem-
ble and advance their respective arguments for papal and
regnal sovereignty at the end of the thirteenth century.[2]

---

1 Broadly, the words *decretal*, *decretalis*, or *epistola decretalis* signify
a pontifical letter containing a *decretum* or pontifical decision.

2 By "directly," I mean glossing the decretal in which an idea was
first introduced. By "indirectly," I mean glossing subsequent decre-

Quanto personam was a papal decretal that nominally dealt with the authority to translate a bishop from one episcopal see to another. The proximate cause for its transmission was Bishop Conrad of Querfort's unilateral decision to transfer himself from Hildesheim's see to the more affluent see of Würzburg. Viewing this transfer as a violation of what he considered the exclusively papal prerogative to translate bishops, Innocent III responded by instructing Conrad to quit both Würzburg and his former see of Hildesheim. *Quanto personam*, issued on August 21, 1198, ordered a group of five German bishops to enforce this command by excommunicating Conrad from the Church if he failed to comply with the papal mandate to vacate both sees within twenty days. The decretal was incorporated into Innocent's authoritative collection, *Compilatio tertia*, in 1209/10 and was subsequently glossed by several influential canonists, including Laurentius Hispanus, Vincentius Hispanus, Johannes Teutonicus, and Tancred. Although Innocent issued several decretals on unauthorized episcopal translations, *Quanto personam* is generally considered to be the most consequential.

Innocent's decretal makes several claims regarding the locus and character of supreme authority within the Church. Concerning the locus of supreme authority, the decretal clearly asserts that such authority is vested in the papal office. In condemning Conrad's unauthorized translation from Hildesheim's see to that of Würzburg, Innocent argued that a bishop is married to his see and may not leave that see unless the marital bond had been dissolved. As only God, he maintained, was able to dissolve the bond of marriage, so only God was able to dissolve the episcopal marriage of a bishop to his see. Innocent then asserted that the pope is the "vicar of Christ"—that is, Christ's deputy or agent on Earth—and that the pope, therefore, is exclusively empowered to sever the bond of episcopal marriage and translate a bishop from one see to another.[3]

---

tals in which the idea was reused or refined; compilations of decretals; or earlier glosses.

3 Innocent III was not the first to use the title Vicar of Christ.

In conceptualizing the pope as the sole "Vicar of Christ," Innocent thus echoed Bernard of Clairvaux's claim that the papal office was the sole locus of supreme authority within the Church. The pope did not share the title with the episcopate, nor were the bishops vicars of Christ in their own right. Instead, the pope stood above the bishops, in the place of Christ, wielding supreme power within the Church. But Innocent went far beyond the abbot of Clairvaux, by reconceptualizing the very nature of supreme power vested in the papal office. In making his case against Conrad, Innocent distinguished between two types of power wielded by the pope. On the one hand, he argued, both popes and bishops possessed what he called "ordinary" authority—that is, legitimate power derived from, and limited by, human law, tradition, and custom. On the other hand, Innocent argued that the pope, by virtue of his being the vicar of Christ, also possessed an extraordinary form of authority—which he labelled "divine" authority. This authority, reserved exclusively to the papal office, allowed popes to exercise Christ's extraordinary prerogative to transcend human law, tradition, and custom in certain circumstances. Innocent expressed the pope's exclusive divine authority in the following terms:

> God, not man, separates a bishop from his Church because the Roman pontiff dissolves the bond between them by divine rather than human authority, carefully considering each translation's need and usefulness. The pope has this authority because he does not exercise the office of man, but of the true God on earth.[4]

Peter Damian had applied it to the pope in 1057, and, in his *De consideratione* (ca. 1150), Bernard of Clairvaux had also declared the pope *Vicarius Christi*. See: Agostino Paravicini Bagliani, *The Pope's Body*, trans. David S. Peterson (Chicago: University of Chicago Press, 2000), 58–59.

4 Kenneth Pennington, *Pope and Bishops: The Papal Monarchy in the Twelfth and Thirteenth Centuries* (Philadelphia: University of Pennsylvania Press, 1984), 16.

In conceptualizing the pope's power in this way, Innocent thus added a further dimension to the idea of papal fullness of power (*plenitudo potestatis*). By the time Innocent was elected pope, the meaning of this term had largely been fixed in decretist thought. When used in connection with its adjunct concept of shared care of the Church (*in partem sollicitudinis*), it highlighted the difference between the pope's universal jurisdiction and a bishop's merely local jurisdiction. When detached from its adjunct, the term conveyed a sense of papal legislative omnicompetence and judicial primacy (in the language of Roman law *papa est iudex ordinarius omnium*).[5] Moreover, by the end of the twelfth century, *plenitudo potestatis* had also come to imply that the partial and lesser jurisdictional powers of the bishops were derived from the fuller and greater jurisdictional authority of the pope. In *Quanto personam*, however, Innocent invested it with an additional layer of meaning: for Innocent, the idea of papal *plenitudo potestatis* also entailed a claim that the pope both shared in, and exercised, the divine power of God Himself.

Canon lawyers at the university of Bologna developed the ideas that Innocent had introduced in *Quanto personam* in several ways. Laurentius Hispanus, in one of the decretal's earliest glosses, initiated this process by taking up the question of the limits of papal *plenitudo potestatis*. Over the twelfth century, canonists had constructed a doctrine of papal primacy that emphasized the pope's supreme authority to command, legislate, and judge within the institutional Church. Significantly, this doctrine did not construe papal supreme authority as being unconstrained or absolute. For example, popes were not permitted to change the unwritten constitution of the Church, the *status ecclesiae*. Nor were they

---

5 J. A. Watt. "The Theory of the Papal Monarchy in the Thirteenth Century: The Contribution of the Canonists," *Traditio* 20 (1964): 179–317. See also Watt, "The Use of the Term *plenitudo potestatis* in Hostiensis," in *Proceedings of the Second International Congress of Medieval Canon Law*, ed. S. Kuttner and J. J. Ryan (Vatican City: Congregatio de Seminariis et Studiorum Universitatibus, 1965), 161–87.

permitted to alienate the rights attached to the papal office. Nor, significantly, were they permitted to legislate arbitrarily. The pope's legislative authority was limited by the principle that to be valid, any laws he promulgated had to correspond to both justice and reason. Twelfth-century canonists like Huguccio simply could not imagine that a law could be legally binding unless it were both just and reasonable—that is, in accord with natural and divine law as apprehended by human reason or revealed in scripture. Human-made laws had to reflect the higher norms of natural and divine law, otherwise they were considered not to be laws at all.

It was this last limitation that Laurentius was to reconceptualize, in the process inadvertently laying the foundations for the later development of the idea of both positive law and absolute power. As Kenneth Pennington has argued,[6] underpinning the conception of papal authority prevailing before Laurentius' time was a tension between two understandings of royal power. On the one hand, there was a current of Roman jurisprudence that viewed the prince as the source of the law ("what pleases the prince has the force of law") and his power as therefore unlimited ("the prince is not bound by the law"). On the other hand, there was the view—expressed in another current of Roman law and Germanic law and feudal custom—that while the prince may be the source of the law, he was not free to enact any law he pleased. Law, to be valid, had to be just and reasonable. By the time of Huguccio, this tension had been resolved in canonist thought by arguing that the will of the pope had the force of law because his will was informed by reason. The ultimate source of the law, they assumed, was thus reason, not merely the prince's unconstrained will.

Laurentius' revolutionary move was to gloss *Quanto personam* in such a way as to invert this formula. Motivated by

---

6 Kenneth Pennington, "Law, Legislative Authority, and Theories of Government, 1150–1300," in *The Cambridge History of Medieval Political Thought c. 350–c. 1450*, ed. J. H. Burns (Cambridge: Cambridge University Press, 1988), 424–53, at 427–30.

a desire to enhance papal legislative authority to "overcome the vast mass of worldly and often corrupt customs that dominated the life of the church," he asserted that no longer was the pope's will *informed* by reason; it *was* reason.[7] As Laurentius put it,

> [The pope] is said to have a divine will.... O, how great is the power of the prince; he changes the nature of things by applying the essences of one thing to another.... He can make iniquity from justice by correcting any canon or law, for in these things his will is held to be reason....[8]

The consequences of Laurentius' inversion of the prevailing canonist formula were twofold. First, he decisively established that one source of the law was the prince's will. In claiming that the pope's "will is held to be reason" (*pro ratione voluntas*), Laurentius was arguing that in certain circumstances, the pope's "divine will" could substitute for reason as the font of legitimate law. Typically, positive law (*ius positivum*) was grounded in reason. Occasionally, however, a law promulgated by the prince was not consonant with reason. On these occasions, the prince's will substituted for reason as the underlying source of that law's validity. Second, Laurentius' inversion introduced a new way of thinking about the content of the law. Whereas the prevailing view at the time was that positive law, to be valid, had to reflect natural or divine law, Laurentius asserted that there was no necessary correlation between them. If the pope could change what was previously held to be just into an iniquity, then obviously positive law was not necessarily an expression of unchanging natural or divine law. Indeed, Laurentius' gloss strongly implied that positive law was nothing more than a human ordinance legislated by a competent authority. It also implied that a competent authority had the power to enact laws that

---

7 Brian Tierney, *Origins of Papal Infallibility, 1150-1350: A Study on the Concepts of Infallibility, Sovereignty, and Tradition in the Middle Ages* (Leiden: Brill, 1972), 29.

8 Pennington, *The Prince and the Law*, 47.

were neither just nor reasonable in the traditional sense. Of course, none of this suggests that Laurentius understood the pope's legislative power to be completely unbridled. The concluding words of the passage quoted above are, "He is held, nevertheless, to shape his power to the public good." Moreover, the goal of the canonists at this time was to enhance the pope's authority to repeal old laws and enact new ones—not to challenge the "permanent truths" of scripture or to set the pope above them.[9] Instead, it is to argue that Laurentius' gloss on *Quanto personam* identified the pope as the ultimate wellspring of legislative authority within the Church and thus conferred on him unprecedented freedom when enacting positive law for the good of the Church.

In the decades after Laurentius, several other canonists also glossed *Quanto personam*. In the course of glossing the *Compilationes antiquae* between 1210 and 1220 and the *Decretals of Gregory IX* in 1234 (both of which included *Quanto personam*), the canonist Vincentius Hispanus reiterated Laurentius' main claim that the source of legislative authority within the Church was the pope's will. But although in broad agreement with his countryman, Vincentius departed from Laurentius in several essential respects. First, rather than ground the prince's legislative authority in canon law, he grounded it in Roman law, citing both the *Institutes* (1.2.6) and the Roman jurist Ulpian (*Digest* 1.4.1), to the effect that, "What pleases the prince has the force of law." Similarly, Vincentius agreed with Laurentius that the prince's power was not absolute, but once again grounded his argument in Roman law. Specifically, he cited *Digna vox*, a text in which the emperor, while legally "loosed from the laws" (*legibus solutus*), by his own will chose to observe those laws. Applying this logic to the papal office, he concluded that the pope was thus "bound by the laws of the Church and his duty to rule the clergy and churches according to the canons, all for the maintenance of the faith and the *status Ecclesiae*, just as the emperor was bound by the laws of the state" (Post,

---

9 Tierney, *Origins of Papal Infallibility*, 30–31.

"Vincentius Hispanus," p. 168). Finally, as Gaines Post has argued, Vincentius was the first to apply *pro ratione voluntas* to temporal princes as well as the pope.[10]

Johannes Teutonicus, writing ca. 1216, also explored the idea of *pro ratione voluntas* but developed it differently. In the course of enumerating several examples of situations in which the pope's will was held to be reason, he argued that the pope "exercises the office of God because he makes something out of nothing...."[11] As Pennington has argued, although the phrase "makes something of nothing" proved confusing to both the early modern editors of the *Corpus iuris canonici* and some modern historians, its meaning is actually quite clear. Johannes, Pennington argues, was not suggesting that the pope possessed miraculous or divine powers to create things *ex nihilo*. Rather, he was punning on the Latin word *nulla*, which can mean "nothing" or "invalid," to make the more modest case that a prince had the power to validate legal judgments that were otherwise invalid, and that when he exercises that power he can be said to have made something out of nothing. In the context of papal authority, Johannes was thus arguing that the pope had the power to validate an invalid decision of an ecclesiastical court, a point he made explicit in a later gloss of the *Compilation tertia* when he argued that the pope "can suspend the effect [of excommunication]...for he makes a valid from an invalid judgment...."[12] Therefore, the pope could "recognize the deposition of a bishop by a court even though the deposition was [technically] invalid because the court did not have jurisdictions over the deposition of bishops...."[13] Like Laurentius and Vincentius, Johannes was not arguing that the pope had

---

10 Gaines Post, "Vincentius Hispanus, 'pro ratione voluntas' and Medieval and Early Modern Theories of Sovereignty," *Traditio* 28 (1972): 159–84.

11 Pennington, *Pope and Bishops*, 26.

12 Pennington, *Pope and Bishops*, 28.

13 Pennington, *Pope and Bishops*, 28.

unbridled, arbitrary, or absolute power to create law or render judgment. Instead, he was making the case that part of the papal prerogative entailed in *pro ratione voluntas* was the power to make lawful episcopal decisions or judgments that were legally deficient in some way if it served the public good.

However, if the decretists Laurentius, Vincentius, and Johannes understood the pope's legislative and judicial powers to be strictly limited, Tancred, perhaps the greatest of the early decretalists, offered a decidedly less restrained interpretation. In his commentary on *Quanto personam*, he stated that the pope was the vicar of God and thus acted in place of God in ecclesiastical affairs. In this capacity, Tancred asserted, the pope enjoyed *plenitudo potestatis* and could, therefore, correct, change, or even dispense from positive law according to his will. Being God's vicar, he was above all earthly powers and the law (*supra ius*).

In enumerating papal powers and their sources, Tancred's commentary largely echoed those of Laurentius, Vincentius, and Johannes. However, whereas those jurists had placed strict limits on the pope's power by narrowly delimiting the prerogatives entailed in the doctrine of *pro ratione voluntas* or by subordinating the pope's extraordinary legislative authority to the public good, Tancred imposed only minimal restraints on papal power. Significantly, he did not refer to *Digna vox* or public utility or any of the other strong limiting formulas developed by his predecessors. Rather, when writing about the limits of papal legislative and judicial authority, he simply stated that the pope could not unilaterally change the *status ecclesiae* or act against the articles of catholic faith. But even here, Tancred left it to the pope himself to decide if, in exercising his power, he was changing the *status ecclesiae* or contradicting settled articles of the faith. Overall, Tancred strongly implied that the pope had broad discretion in promulgating and dispensing positive law—certainly far more discretion than Laurentius, Vincentius, and Johannes had afforded the papal office.

In both tone and substance, the hesitations and reservations found in the decretist commentaries on *Quanto personam*

were replaced in Tancred's decretalist commentaries by bold
assertions of papal legislative and judicial authority. To be sure,
Tancred was not espousing a doctrine of unlimited or extreme
absolutism. He clearly believed that the exercise of papal legislative and judicial power was not contingent solely upon the
pope's discretion or will. Instead, Tancred was advocating what
Gaines Post has referred to as a doctrine of "moderate absolutism"—that is, a doctrine that emphasized and endorsed
expansive papal power to legislate, command, and judge, but
that did not break entirely with the traditional decretist view
that there were nevertheless limits to that power.[14]

In the middle decades of the thirteenth century, the concept of *plenitudo potestatis* migrated from the spiritual to the
temporal realm as members of Emperor Frederick II's chan-
cery who had previously served in Innocent's curia, and who
were thus familiar with Innocent's formula, began using it to
define the relationship between the emperor and the princes
of the empire. In this context, *plenitudo potestatis* was reserved
to the emperor, while the *pars sollicitudinis* was conceded to
the princes. Frederick seems to have been attracted to this
formula because it offered him a way to integrate the princes
into an imperial order in which he enjoyed universal jurisdiction and supreme authority, while the princes merely enjoyed
local jurisdiction and derivative authority. Frederick was
probably also attracted to the concept because it provided
him with a framework for reconceptualizing the empire as a
political institution based on a hierarchy of offices rather than
a feudal one based on ties of personal loyalty. Whatever his
motives, in adopting and adapting Innocent's formula, Frederick placed the fullness of power at the disposal not only of all
future emperors but of kings and other temporal rulers as well.

Henricus de Segusio, or Hostiensis as he came to be
known after he was created cardinal-bishop of Ostia in 1262,

---

14 The canonists Bernard of Parma, William Durant, and Goffredus
da Trani all espoused a similar doctrine. Regarding Bernard and
William, see Post, "Vincentius Hispanus, 'pro ratione voluntas',"
173–74.

developed the concept of *plenitudo potestatis* more fully than any of his canonist predecessors. Through commentaries on Innocent III's *Quanto personam*, and on subsequent decretals by Innocent such as *Cum ex illo*, *Inter corporalia*, *Proposuit*, *Magnae devotionis*, and *Cum ad monasterium* (in all of which Innocent applied the core concepts first articulated in *Quanto personam* to different legal cases) he introduced several conceptual innovations that brought the seeds planted by Innocent to full flower. Foundationally, Hostiensis refined and amplified Innocent's idea of *vicarius Christi*. The decretists and early decretalists had not made much of this idea, focusing their attention instead on the idea of *pro ratione voluntas*. However, in Hositiensis' hands, the idea that the pope shared in and exercised Christ's divine authority became the cornerstone of a more unfettered papal absolutism than even Tancred had espoused. His argument was simple, even if typically expressed in extravagant language. All political authority is derived from God; therefore, all who exercise such authority can be said to govern by divine mandate.[15] But the pope's authority, he argued, was qualitatively different from that of other princes. Echoing language used by Innocent and drawing on many of the same texts as Laurentius, Hostiensis argued that the pope did not govern by divine *mandate*; rather, he governed as a divine *agent*. As the vicar of Christ, he acted in Christ's place. Therefore, he concluded in his gloss on *Quanto personam*, whenever the pope acts *de iure*, he exercises Christ's divine authority, and therefore his acts are, *ipso facto*, licit.[16] The only factor limiting the papal exercise of this divine authority was sin: given that Christ was without sin, Hostiensis argued, the pope simply could not be acting in Christ's place if he was acting sinfully.

Upon this understanding of *vicarius Christi*, Hostiensis then developed precise legal concepts to replace Innocent's

---

15 Pennington, *The Prince and the Law*, 51. For the influence of Tancred, see Watt, "The Use of the Term *plenitudo potestatis* in Hostiensis," 166n29.

16 Pennington, *The Prince and the Law*, 51.

vague formulations. Perhaps most importantly, where Innocent had written vaguely about papal *plenitudo potestatis*, and where the decretists had attempted to flesh out Innocent's thought in rhetorically expansive but conceptually imprecise ways, Hostiensis set out to enumerate the specific legal powers inherent in the pope's fullness of power. One way he did this was to attempt to parse the vague phrase "above the law" (*supra ius* or *supra omnia iura*) that had come into increasingly widespread use among the canonists since Innocent's decretal *Proposuit*. According to Hostiensis, the pope could act *supra ius* in two ways. On the one hand, under the doctrine of what he (following Innocent) called *suppletio defectuum*, the pope could make good any deficiency in fact, law, or legal procedure. As Watt put it, the "*suppletio* was an act of the absolute power to remedy defects that had arisen either through the non-observance of existing law or because existing law was inadequate to meet the particular circumstances."[17] On the other hand, Hostiensis argued that the power to act *supra ius* entailed the authority to dispense from the law. Again quoting Watt, dispensation "was a use of the absolute power to set aside existing law."[18] To be sure, Hostiensis believed that the pope required a valid cause or reason to act *supra ius*. But he also believed that ultimately it was the pope himself who had the power to determine whether such cause or reason existed in any given case.

Hostiensis also sought to refine the concept of *plenitudo potestatis* by bringing greater precision to Innocent's somewhat fuzzy concept of papal "divine power." He did so by drawing on the works of early thirteenth-century theologians such as Godfrey of Poitiers, William of Auxerre, and Alexander of Hales who had distinguished between two facets of God's divine power: His absolute power (*potestas absoluta*) and His ordinary power (*potestas ordinata*). According to these theologians, *potestas absoluta* referred to God's abstract or theoretical power to do whatever he pleased, while *potestas ordinata*

---

17 Watt, "The Use of the Term *plenitudo potestatis* in Hostiensis," 167.

18 Watt, "The Use of the Term *plenitudo potestatis* in Hostiensis," 167.

referred to the limited or ordered power He actually chose to exercise.[19] Applying these theological concepts to the idea of papal authority introduced by Innocent in *Quanto personam*, Hostiensis argued that the pope, too, exercised two kinds of power. Here, however, he dramatically altered the meaning of the distinction introduced by the theologians. Where they had understood this distinction as referring to the difference between "what God *could have done* other than things he chose to do," Hostiensis understood the pope's absolute power or *potestas absoluta* as a form of divine power. On this view, the pope's ordinary power or *potestas ordinata* was his human power to act within, and on the basis of, the law, while his *potestas absoluta* was his divine power to transcend the law—that is, his power to act beyond the laws that defined and limited his *potestas ordinata*.[20]

Drawing these two strands of thought together, Hostiensis further elaborated his idea of *potestas absoluta* in his commentaries on two papal decretals, Alexander III's *Ex publico* (dealing with marriage law) and Innocent III's *Cum ad monasterium* (dealing with solemn vows). In the first of these, Hostiensis argued that the pope could "allow a spouse to separate from an unwilling partner by exercising his absolute power." In the second, he made the case that the pope could use his *potestas absoluta* to dispense from the monastic rule, but only with just cause. These commentaries reveal that Hostiensis had come to believe that while the pope could not promulgate divine law and was subject to it, he could dispense from it in certain narrowly prescribed matters. This was a new element of papal *potestas absoluta*. Hostiensis' decretist and even decrelalist predecessors had argued that the pope could, in certain circumstances, supplement or dispense from *positive* law, but none had gone so far as to claim that the

---

19 Pennington, *The Prince and the Law*, 55.

20 The standard history of the evolution of the distinction between absolute and ordained power is still William J. Courtenay, *Capacity, and Volition: A History of the Distinction of Absolute and Ordained Power* (Bergamo: Lubrina, 1990).

pope could dispense from higher law. However, Hostiensis now claimed that as vicar of Christ, the pope could exercise God's authority to set aside natural and divine law pertaining to marriage and religious vows. In subsequent comments on Celestine III's decretal *Sicut unire* (dealing with the pope's power to unite episcopal sees), Hostiensis went even farther, arguing that the power to dispense from divine law was not limited to marriage and vows, but could also be used to regulate the *status ecclesiae* itself.[21] In so doing, he broke with his predecessors, who had argued that the pope was bound by the Church's fundamental constitution and could neither alter nor abolish the *status ecclesiae*.

But if Hostiensis broke with his predecessors regarding the specific limits of the papal *potesta absoluta*, he did not break with them regarding the general principle that papal power was, in fact, limited. For Hostiensis, the concept of *plenitudo potestatis* did not entail or imply unbridled or arbitrary power. To be sure, as Innocent had argued in his decretal *Proposuit*, Hostiensis believed that the pope's *potesta absoluta* allowed him to act *supra ius* with respect to positive law solely on the basis of his will. However, even Hostiensis accepted that the pope could only act above natural or divine law "with cause."[22] As he put it in his commentary on Innocent III's decretal *Magnae devotionis*, "If cause is not present, or is not sufficient, it is not proper for [the pope] to deviate from the law."[23] And like other jurists of the era,

---

[21] For an extended discussion of Hostiensis's views on *potesta absoluta*, see Pennington, *Pope and Bishops*, 65-73; Pennington, *The Prince and the Law*, 49-75; and Watt, "The Use of the Term *plenitudo potestatis* in Hostiensis," 161-75.

[22] In other words, with a valid reason. In the medieval context, a valid reason was typically understood as one that promoted the "utility of the state and especially the Church...," Pennington, *The Prince and the Law*, 64. Hostiensis is thus arguing that the pope could only act *supra ius* if it were necessary for the public good (*utilitas publica*).

[23] Pennington, *The Prince and the Law*, 62-63.

Hostiensis also believed that, although not bound by the law, the pope should nevertheless subject himself to it, except on rare occasions.

In *Quanto personam* and its glosses, Innocent and the canonists made a number of significant contributions to the idea of supreme authority—ideas that would eventually be picked up by early modern thinkers like Bodin and worked into their theories of sovereignty. The pope established that the papal office was the sole locus of supreme authority within the Church and that, as vicar of Christ, the pope alone exercised what he called "divine power" on earth. Building on this, the canonists began reimagining the legal character of papal authority, first by locating the source of canon law in the will of the pope and then by loosing the pope from almost all of the constraints of positive, natural and divine law (at least in certain circumstances). In the process, they developed and refined several concepts—*pro ratione voluntas*, *plenitudo potestatis*, *potesta absoluta*—that were to migrate to the political realm and have long and fruitful careers in the history of Latin Christian political thought. In the shorter term, they also furnished succeeding generations of medieval jurists, polemicists, theologians, and philosophers with the intellectual resources they would need to fashion a distinctively medieval—yet simultaneously proto-modern—concept of sovereignty at the turn of the fourteenth century.

Chapter 2

The Locus of Supreme Authority
Per venerabilem

In this chapter I trace the evolution of juristic thought regarding the proper locus of supreme authority. I do this by examining how an idea introduced in the influential papal decretal *Per venerabilem* was received, re-worked, and re-interpreted over the course of the thirteenth century, in the process generating a concept of specifically *regnal* sovereignty—a concept that would be taken up by the intellectual protagonists in the conflict between Boniface and Philip, and that would provide John of Paris with an important element of his theory of sovereignty at the turn of the fourteenth century.

Per venerabilem was a papal decretal that nominally dealt with the pope's power to legitimize illegitimate children, not so that they could enter holy orders (which was established precedent), but so that they could inherit property. The proximate cause for the transmission of this decretal was a petition from Count William of Montpellier requesting that Innocent legitimize the children born of his mistress. Ordinarily, the count would have submitted this petition to his temporal superior, the king of France. In this case, however, William did not want to compromise his *de facto* independence from the French crown by formally submitting such a petition; nor did he wish to undermine Montpellier's close commercial and diplomatic relations with the Spanish kingdom of Aragon by formally acknowledging his vassalage to the king of France. Having no other option, he appealed to Innocent, recalling in his petition that the pope had already legitimized the children of the illicit union of King Philip Augustus and Agnes of Meran.

In response to this appeal, in 1202, Pope Innocent III issued *Per venerabilem*. This decretal was structured around two basic lines of argumentation. Narrowly, it dealt with the specifics of William's plea. Citing a number of factual and legal differences between William's case and that of Philip Augustus, Innocent rejected William's request outright. But that was not the end of the matter. More broadly, *Per venerabilem* made the case that, although William's specific plea was found wanting, the pope nevertheless possessed the general right to decide such issues—that is, to act in temporal matters. In the course of making both his narrow and broad claims, Innocent injected into canon law a set of arguments, assertions, and assumptions that would have a long and fruitful career in the history of medieval political thought. And he made certain that this would be the case by ensuring that the decretal was included in the official collection of canon law known as the *Compilatio tertia*, and also in the curriculum of the influential university of Bologna.

Per venerabilem would reverberate down through the Middle Ages for two reasons, only one of which is directly germane to the evolution of the idea of sovereignty. First, the decretal was a historically consequential assertion of papal jurisdiction in the temporal sphere, both in claiming for the apostolic see the narrow right to legitimate illegitimate children in temporal matters and in claiming for itself appellate jurisdiction in both spiritual and temporal matters. Second, and for the purposes of this study more importantly, the decretal initiated a long line of argumentation regarding the universality or otherwise of the emperor's political jurisdiction. One of the arguments that William had relied on was the precedent set by the case of King Philip Augustus of France, which had resulted in the pope legitimizing the illegitimate children of the French king for the purposes of succession. But Innocent responded to William's claim that this earlier case was a precedent by pointing to a number of factual and legal differences between the two cases. One of these differences, and a minor one at that, was that whereas the king of France recognized no temporal superior to whom he could appeal, William did. But while only a relatively minor element of Innocent's response, and in a sense nothing more than an expression of an obvious truth, this was to prove monumentally consequential. For in stating that the king of France recognized no superior, Innocent was also asserting or implying that kings *in general* recognize no superior (*rex qui superiorem non recognoscit*) and that the king is emperor in his own kingdom (*rex in regno suo est imperator regni sui*). Both of these ideas, in vesting supreme authority in kings rather than popes or emperors, would prove foundational to the emerging conceptual structure of regnal sovereignty. As both of these ideas quickly became fused in the medieval mind –in commentary on canon, civil, and customary law—I will treat them in a single narrative under the banner of regnal sovereignty.

Against this backdrop of perennial conflicts over the locus of supreme authority among popes, emperors, and kings over the course of the thirteenth century, Innocent's apparently inconsequential observation that the king of France recognized no superior in temporal matters in a decretal about legitimizing children was perhaps fated to have a long and deeply consequential career. It was decisively launched on that career around the year 1208 when the canonist Alanus Anglicus produced one of its earliest glosses. In the service of his broader project of promoting the hierocratic view of papal supremacy and denying the emperor the status of *dominus mundi*, Alanus extracted from Innocent's decretal the principle of *unusquisque enim tantum juris habet in regno suo, quantum imperator in imperio* (for each [king] has a such right in his own kingdom as the emperor in the empire), clearly implying that the king is emperor in his kingdom—*rex in regno suo est imperator*. Addressing Innocent's decretal in his *Apparatus* of glosses to the *Decretum*, he did this in two ways. First he argued that, just as the *lex regia* conferred supreme temporal authority on the emperor in the empire, so too it conferred such authority on a king in his kingdom. And second, he made a parallel argument that, just as the emperor had legitimate authority to declare war (the exclusive preserve of those wielding supreme authority), so too did those princes who recognized no superior temporal authority (i.e., kings). The logic in both cases was the same: in not recognizing the superior authority of the emperor, kings became peers of the emperor and thus came to possess all the same powers as the emperor. In such cases, Alanus reasoned, just as the *lex regia* conferred sovereignty upon the emperor in his empire, so too it conferred sovereignty upon the king in his kingdom. The authority of kings was not derived from that of the emperor, but identical in kind and degree to it. While Alanus made allowances for papal intervention in temporal affairs by reason of sin (*ratione peccati*), and conceded that the pope therefore enjoyed a kind of superiority over all temporal powers, he implicitly rejected both the right of the emperor to intervene in the affairs of kings and the need of kings to seek authorization from the emperor for sovereign acts such as declaring war. The only question, both unasked and unanswered in Alanus' work, was whether the sovereignty of kings was *de iure* or merely *de facto*.

While not considered by Alanus, however, from the time it was introduced by Bernardus Compostellanus Antiquus, this distinction structured much of the thirteenth-century discourse regarding the locus of supreme political authority. On one hand, those who sided with the emperor in his ongoing struggles for supremacy with popes and kings tended to argue that while some kings might not *recognize* imperial sovereignty, that was merely a brute political fact and not a legal reality. These thinkers—mostly, but not exclusively, civil jurists—took seriously the concepts of *rex qui superiorem non recognoscit* and *rex in regno suo est imperator regni sui*. But they did so in a specific way and with a specific political purpose in mind. For those who were invested in the imperial project, the goal was to accommodate these new ideas to a legal framework that retained the emperor as the source and summit of political authority within the empire.

Among the civil jurists, perhaps the best exemplar of this line of thought is Jacques de Révigny, who taught at the university of Orleans ca. 1270–1290. In rebutting the arguments of Jean de Blanot, a *magister* in the *studium* of law at Bologna, Révigny made the case that while the crime of treason could be committed against the king of France, that did not make the king a *princeps* within the meaning of Roman law. Blanot, of course, had argued the opposite. In his *Commentaria super titulum de actionibus*, written ca. 1256, he had made the case that as the French king had absolute jurisdiction over all the inhabitants of his realm anyone who rebelled against him would be guilty of treason under Roman law. As Blanot put it, such a rebellious subject would be considered treasonous because "he is deemed to have acted directly against the *princeps*, for the king of France is a *princeps* in his own kingdom, since he does not recognize a superior in temporal matters." In Blanot's eyes, the king of France was the supreme political authority in France, *de iure* and *de facto*, and therefore possessed the same *majestas* as the emperor. As he put it in his *Tracatus de actionibus*, "rex in regno suo princeps est" (The king in his kingdom is the *princeps*"). This being the case, he considered any rebellion against the king to be, not an act of feudal infidelity, but *crimen laesae majestatis* or the crime of treason. Révigny, on the other hand, saw things quite differently. For him, a rebellious subject of the French king would indeed be guilty of treason, but not because the king possessed the *majestas* that would make him the object of such a crime. Rather, such a rebellious subject would be guilty of treason "because the crime is committed against a magistrate of the *princeps* [emperor], for France and Spain have once been and therefore shall always be under the empire."[1] For Révigny, the king of France unquestionably enjoyed some form of *de facto* independence from the emperor. And he certainly could be the object of the crime of treason. But Révigny could not concede that the

---

1 S. H. Cuttler, *The Law of Treason and Treason Trials in Later Medieval France* (Cambridge: Cambridge University Press, 1982), 11.

French king was *de iure* anything but a subject and magistrate of the emperor.

Johannes Teutonicus came to similar conclusions regarding the locus of supreme temporal authority, but arrived at them via the logic of canon, rather than civil, law. Johannes' principal political commitment was to the ideal of a unified empire ruled by the emperor as *dominus mundi*. In his glosses of both *Per venerabilem* and *Venerabilem fratrem* he concedes that *de facto* the king of France recognizes no superior, but insists that *de iure* France remains part and parcel of the empire, subject to the supreme authority of the emperor and Roman law. Elsewhere he states categorically that the emperor is *dominus mundi*, lord of all kings and lesser princes. And in another work, he characterizes France and Spain as mere "provinces" of the empire. Even Johannes, however, is forced to at least gesture in the direction of *de iure* sovereignty for Spain, largely on the grounds that they "snatched the kingdom from the jaws of the enemy when they were not subject to the empire."[2] Ultimately, even though he adopted the *de facto/de iure* distinction and other elements of the emerging discourse of regnal sovereignty, he remained committed to the view that supreme political authority is vested *de iure* in the emperor, the *dominus mundi*.

Those seeking to shift the locus of supreme authority decisively in favour of kings, on the other hand, either because they were in the service of those kings or because they were hierocrats seeking to diminish the status of the emperor vis-à-vis the pope in any way they could, adopted a view less deferential to the emperor and his prerogatives. For these advocates of regnal sovereignty—mostly jurists in the traditions of canon and customary law—the non-recognition of imperial claims, and the associated assertion that kings were emperors in their kingdoms, were not *merely* assertions of political reality. They were understood to be that, to be sure, but they were also viewed as something more—as *legal*

---

2 Gaines Post, "Two Notes on Nationalism in the Middle Ages," *Traditio* 9 (1953): 281–320, at 300.

realities, derived from canon, common, or customary law. Whether commenting directly on *Per venerabilem*, Innocent's other political decretals (*Venerabilem fratrem, Novit*, etc.), or the relevant *dicta* of other jurists, these thinkers developed the argument that supreme temporal authority was legally vested in the kings of independent kingdoms, not in the emperor as head of a universal empire.

Among the first to develop such an argument was Vincentius Hispanus, an influential Spanish decretalist active in the early decades of the thirteenth century. Commenting on Johannes Teutonicus' pro-imperial response to *Per venerabilem*, he argued that Spain is different from all the other provinces of Christendom in that it alone successfully resisted Charlemagne's efforts to incorporate it into his empire. To Vincentius, this implied not only that Spain had the right similarly to resist Charles' then-ongoing efforts to make it part of the Holy Roman Empire, but that it was an empire in its own right, separate and distinct from that dominated by the German emperors so beloved of Johannes Teutonicus. His glosses on the *Decretals of Innocent III* and his *Apparatus* to the *Decretals of Gregory IX* reflect a similar line of reasoning—that whatever conversations were taking place within the rest of Latin Christendom regarding the relative powers of kings and emperors, they had nothing to do with "Blessed Lady Spain." In Vincentius' eyes, Spain was an empire unto itself, defined by its Visigothic patrimony, its successful history of resistance and *reconquista*, and its own imperial lineage, culminating in Alfonso VI. It was, in effect, a sovereign kingdom, independent of, and equal to, that of the Germans.[3]

Vincentius was clearly an advocate for Spanish exceptionalism. Most canonists, however, were not particularly interested in Spanish claims to *de iure* regnal sovereignty. Rather, the impetus driving most of their theorizing about the *de iure* nature of regnal sovereignty was some legal issue related to France. To be sure, the canonists often expressed themselves in terms that were generalizable. But the king of

---

3 Post, "Two Notes on Nationalism," 306–8.

France, and his relationship to the emperor, was either the proximate cause at hand or the backdrop against which that proximate cause was being considered.

Three canonists in particular exemplify this broader concern with the powers of kings as such. The first of these was Innocent IV, pope from 1243 to 1254. Innocent's pontificate was defined in large measure by his conflict with Emperor Frederick II over issues as perennial as the nature of the relationship between the temporal and spiritual powers and as fleeting as the geopolitical balance on the Italian peninsula. This conflict inclined Innocent to seek to diminish the standing of the emperor and to support the French king and others in their efforts to assert their independence, *de facto* and *de iure*, from the empire. It is hardly surprising, then, that he took up the ideas of regnal sovereignty then circulating and deployed them against the emperor when and where he could. Sometimes, this took the form of seemingly trivial arguments like the one he made against the prevailing view that only the emperor had the right to create notaries. In this case, Innocent argued against the prevailing view that the emperor alone possessed this power that "Credimus tamen, quod alii reges, qui habent supremum et merum imperium, possent idem statuere ce tabellionibus, si vellent" (We believe, however, that the other kings who have supreme and pure authority are also able to create notaries, if they wish). But it could also take the form of the obviously significant argument that kings lawfully possessed the authority to declare war. Against the presumption that only the emperor possessed such authority, Innocent declared in his *Apparatus* on the *Decretal* of Gregory IX that "Bellum autem secundum quod proprie dicitur solus princeps qui superiorem non habet indicere potest" (War properly called, however, can only be declared by a prince who has no superior).[4] At one level, this was a notable contribution to just war theory, as the decretists had usually been uncertain about which temporal authorities

---

4 On Innocent IV's analysis of war, see Russell, *The Just War in the Middle Ages* (Cambridge: Cambridge University Press, 1977).

had the authority to declare wars in an era where the law still seemed to vest that power exclusively in the emperor but where the concrete realities made that difficult to sustain. But it was also a notable contribution to the evolving theory of regnal sovereignty. For it decisively established, in canon law but with knock-on effects in civil law, that there were temporal powers that did not recognize the superordinate authority of the emperor, and that these powers were deemed *de iure* to posses the ultimate temporal authority—the authority to wage war. As this power had previously been at least partly derivative of imperial sovereignty, its translation to kings was in significant measure definitive of the evolving theory and reality of regnal sovereignty. Tellingly, the language Innocent used to make this argument was redolent of that introduced by his predecessor in *Per venerabilem*.

Guilelmus Durandus, in his encyclopedic treatise of canon law (and, to some extent, civil law) the *Speculum iudiciale* (first published 1271–1276), also develops the idea that the king of France is the legal equal of the emperor. His approach, however, differed from that of the pope. Durandus' concern was not with the question of who could lawfully declare war, but rather with the equally freighted question of whether a rebellious lord could be guilty of the crime of treason (*crimen laesae majestatis*). In the *Corpus iuris civilis*, only those stubbornly or willfully disobedient to the emperor's authority could be guilty of this crime. It was a crime against the emperor as the ultimate source and summit of political authority. But Durandus argued that a contumacious baron acting against the king of France could also be found guilty of *crimen laesae majestatis*. As he put it, echoing Alanus, "rex Franciae est princeps in regno suo" (The king of France is emperor in his kingdom). He grounded this claim in the argument that "Unde omnes homines, qui sunt in regno Franciae, sunt sub potestate et principatu regis Franciae et in eis habet imperium generalis jurisdictionis et potestatis" (All men in the kingdom of France are under the power and primacy of the king of France and over them he holds the imperium of general jurisdiction and power). In other words, the king, like the emperor in Roman law, was a *princeps*, a bearer of the *merum imperium, suprema et generalis iurisdictio*, and *auctoritas suprema*.[5] Thus, not only did Durandus imply that the French king shared with the emperor the quality of "majesty," he also explicitly made rebellion against the king the *de iure* equivalent of rebellion against the emperor in Roman law. To round out the argument for legal equivalence, he then argued that kingdoms like those of France and Spain that are able to impose their own laws are not bound by Roman law, and that there was therefore no recourse to appeals to the emperor. The apex of the legal system within such kingdoms was the king and the king alone. In this, Durandus concluded, they were like emperors within the empire.

A similar sentiment, possibly derived from the works of Innocent IV, can be found in the *Rosarium*, an influential commentary on the *Decretum*, written by the canonist Guido de Baysio, archdeacon of the city of Bologna and chancellor of its famous university. In the section in which he addressed the question of the jurisdictional authority of princes, "Archidiaconus," as de Baysio was known, wrote that "Dicas, quod omnia imperatoris quoad jurisdictiones. Sic et omnia, quae sunt in regno suo, sunt regis quantum ad jurisdictionem generalem" (You could say that all things are the Emperor's so far as jurisdiction. Similarly, all things which are in his own kingdom are the king's so far as general jurisdiction).[6] The king, in other words, has within his kingdom all the political authority that the emperor has within his empire. While the reference is specifically to the king of France, the sentiment is clearly generalized. It applies to all kings who, like the French king, recognize no temporal superior.

Comparable ideas, expressed in a different idiom and grounded in different legal reasoning, can also be found

---

5 Marguerite Boulet-Sautel, "Le *Princeps* de Guillaume Durand," in *Etudes d'histoire du droit canonique dédiées à Gabriel Le Bras*, 2 vols. (Paris: Sirey, 1965), 2:803–13, at 805–6.

6 Walter Ullmann, "The Development of the Medieval Idea of Sovereignty," *The English Historical Review* 64, no. 250 (1949): 1–33, at 9.

within the tradition of civil law. Two thinkers in particular stand out as both reflecting and driving the evolution of the idea that the supreme authority to command, legislate, and judge was vested in kings of rather than the emperor. The first of these is the Neapolitan jurist Marinus da Caramanico. Commenting on the *Constitutiones regum regni Utriusque Siciliae*, around the year 1276 Marinus made a number of arguments related specifically to the Neapolitan king. Grounding his case in the logic of the *ius gentium*, Marinus argued that the natural state of affairs was one in which political authority was originally vested in kings. As he put it, "Longe ante imperium et romanorum genus ex antiquo, scilicet iure gentium quod cum ipso humano genere proditum est, fuerunt regna cognita" (Long before the empire and the Roman race from of old, that is from the *ius gentium* which emerged with the human race itself, kingdoms were recognized and founded).[7] On this view, the Roman Empire was nothing more than an artifact of brute force, its existence grounded in military might rather than legal right. At best, it was a product of civil law, a body of law deemed inferior to the natural law of peoples, the *ius gentium*. Consequently, Marinus argued, as the empire contracted, the original kingdoms that it had forcibly subjugated were able to reemerge and kings to regain their natural rights to rule those kingdoms. Moreover, as this process unfolded, the empire itself became once again nothing more than the kingdom of the Romans—one kingdom among many, and a moderately sized one at that. Understood in this way, it was clear to Marinus that the political authority exercised by kings was in no way inferior to that exercised by the emperor. Both kings and emperors were "princeps" in the meaning of Roman law. And, as such, both had the *de iure* authority to legislate, tax, wage war, and judge legal cases within their respective territories.

---

7 Joseph Canning, "Ideas of the State in Thirteenth and Fourteenth-Century Commentators on the Roman Law," *Transactions of the Royal Historical Society*, ser. 5, 33 (1983): 1–28, at 5.

Also glossing *Constitutiones regum regni Utriusque Siciliae*, as well as the *Libri feudorum* around the turn of the century, the eminent legal scholar Andreas de Isernia made similar arguments in favour of King Robert's claim that he possessed supreme political authority in his kingdom. First, he argued that, as the emperor's claim to be the sole locus of such authority derived from the forcible subjugation of independent kingdoms to imperial rule, when the empire receded so did the reach of his authority. With the collapse of the empire, he reasoned, the world had returned to a pristine, pre-imperial, condition in which sovereignty had reverted to those once-independent kingdoms that had for a discrete period of time been subject to Roman rule. Second, Isernias argued that supreme political power was in some cases vested in kings who had never recognized a superior in the form of the emperor. As their kingdoms had never been subject to imperial rule, or had been exempted from it for a century or more, the emperor's writ could not now be said to run in their territories. Such kings were presumed to be independent of the emperor and exempt from his authority. Finally, Isernia simply asserted that "Rex est monarcha in regno suo" (The king is monarch in his kingdom), an obvious minor reworking of *rex in regno suo est imperator*. As such, he argued, they had the same *de iure* authority as emperors within the empire ("Liberi reges habent illud jus, quod Romani principes"): the right to mint coins, impose taxes, collects tolls, write laws, dispense justice, create magistrates, wage wars, and so on. They could also be the object of the crime of treason. Isernia rounded out his argument by adverting to Christian scripture, pointing out that as kings were held to be the supreme temporal authority in the Old Testament, so they should always be. For him, "emperor" was nothing more than a pretentious title assumed by one particular king, one who ruled a territorially limited kingdom (which he pretentiously called an empire) that was no different in kind from any other kingdom ruled by any other king.

While focused on the specific cases of France and Naples, all of these arguments regarding the *de iure* locus of supreme authority were generalizable. Unlike the canonist Vincentius' exceptionalist case for Spanish legal independence, which was limited in scope and applicability strictly to Spain, the arguments developed pursuant to the French and Neapolitan cases were implicitly, and sometimes explicitly, applicable to any kingdom ruled by a king who recognized no superior. In other words, while they may have been about the legal independence of the French or Neapolitan kingdoms in a proximate sense, they were ultimately about the *de iure* sovereignty of kingdoms *tout court*.

Finally, we may turn to the case for regnal sovereignty made by Henry of Bracton. Working in the tradition of English customary law, though aware of broader developments in canon and civil law, Bracton argued that within the kingdom of England the English king was without peer or superior. While he was subordinate to the law of the land and governed with the counsel of his earls and barons, his authority came proximately from the people (via the coronation oath, which he considered the equivalent of the *lex regia*) but ultimately from God. The king's *imperium* was thus absolute. Beyond his kingdom, the king of England also recognized no superior other than God and the natural law. In his dealings with other princes who recognized no superior, disputes were to be resolved by petition (or perhaps war), not by petition or appeal to the emperor. As he consistently argued in connection with both internal and external sovereignty, the king has all the rights, dignities, and powers of the emperor (in Roman law) and therefore has supreme and undiluted power to legislate, govern, and judge in the temporal domain.

In glossing *Per venerabilem* and inserting that gloss into his influential compilation, Alanus launched the idea that supreme political authority was vested in kings rather than the emperor onto a long and fruitful career. Motivated by various political projects and drawing resources from a variety of legal traditions, thirteenth-century jurists asserted and argued that supreme temporal authority was vested in neither popes nor emperors, but kings. They did this in two ways. First, they made the case that kings were not subject to the emperor ("rex qui superiorem non recognoscit"). Sometimes they made a *de facto* argument, sometimes a *de jure* one. But either way, the arguments they made fatally undermined the prevailing belief that the ultimate repository of legitimate political power, the sole locus of supreme temporal authority, was the emperor. Second, they made the case that kings were like emperors within their kingdoms ("rex in regno suo est imperator regni sui"). This amounted to a claim that all the temporal powers granted to the emperor in both civil law and the prevailing political imagination were actually vested in kings, not just in practice but in theory as well. In the medium term, these intermingled currents of theorizing the locus of supreme authority provided turn-of-the-fourteenth-century thinkers and polemicists with some of the raw materials they needed to forge a coherent theory of regnal sovereignty. In that sense, there is a direct line from *Per venerabilem* to the full-blown theories of regnal sovereignty articulated by John of Paris, and later by Andreas de Isernia, Oldradus de Ponte, and Marsilius of Padua. In the longer term, the ideas contained within this line of thinking would be picked up by early modern thinkers, combined with other thirteenth- and fourteenth-century ideas regarding the source and character of supreme authority, and fashioned into their own theories of national sovereignty.

Chapter 3

Conflict over Taxation

The late-thirteenth-century conflict between Pope Boniface VIII and the French King Philip IV provided the context within which the medieval idea of sovereignty fully crystallized. It began innocently enough. In the later decades of that century, King Philip began taxing members of the French clergy to help finance his war against England. While formally prohibited by a decree of the Fourth Lateran Council (1215), the papacy had long acquiesced in the practice of French lay rulers taxing their clergy without explicit papal authorization, mainly because it depended on French support in its perennial conflicts with the Holy Roman Emperor. In 1296, however, Boniface decided to apply the prohibition to France as well as the Empire. Historians disagree as to why he made this fateful decision. On the one hand, there are those who assert that the new pope was simply acting on the basis of his firmly held hierocratic belief that ecclesiastical power was superior to temporal power. On this view, Phillip's decision to tax the French Church presented Boniface with his first real opportunity to assert ecclesiastical authority—an opportunity he seized enthusiastically.

On the other hand, some emphasize the role played by Boniface's ardent desire to launch a crusade to recover the Holy Land. From this perspective, the pope's decision had less to do with his hierocratic vision and more with his belief that clerical tax revenues should not be used to sustain a war between Christian rulers, especially when that war was keeping those rulers from "taking the cross" and fighting to liberate the Holy Land. Whatever his motivation, in February 1296 Boniface issued the bull *Clericis laicos*, expressly prohibiting all lay rulers—including "emperors, kings or princes, dukes, counts or barons, podestas, captains or officials or rectors—by whatever name they are called..."—from exacting or receiving ecclesiastical revenues or property without prior authorization from the Apostolic See. The bull also specified the consequences of such unauthorized taxation of the clergy: guilty *persons* were subject to the punishment of excommunication; guilty *corporations* were subject to the punishment of interdict.

Perhaps predictably, Philip responded swiftly to what he perceived to be Boniface's threat to both his political authority and his ability to prosecute his war against England. Within a few months of the promulgation of *Clerics laicos*, Philip issued a royal ordinance forbidding the export of "horses, arms, money, and similar things" from the kingdom. Given the dependence of the papacy on revenues from France, this ordinance put Boniface in an increasingly difficult position. When Philip increased the pressure by issuing a proclamation (never promulgated) obliging the French clergy to contribute its fair share to the public purse and asserting the revocable character of ecclesiastical immunities, Boniface found himself in an utterly untenable position. In an effort to placate Philip, the pope then issued a second bull, *Ineffabilis amor*, in which he explained that *Clericis laicos* had never been intended to forbid "voluntary" donations to the royal coffers or prohibit exactions necessary for the defence of the realm. This was not enough to mollify Philip, however. In 1297, Boniface's deteriorating position in Italy forced him to concede Philip's terms and explicitly recognize the French king's right to tax the French clergy. In a humiliating reversal, the pope issued yet another papal bull, *Esti de statu*, which exempted the French king from the provisions of *Clericis laicos* and conferred upon him the right to tax the French Church without prior papal permission. Satisfied that he had secured his rights and revenues, Philip subsequently withdrew his ordinance forbidding the export of gold and silver, effectively bringing the conflict to an end.

This conflict between Boniface and Philip over taxation gave rise to lines of inquiry regarding the relationship between the spiritual and temporal powers that, if not quite new, certainly had novel dimensions. Were the spiritual and temporal authorities separate and distinct domains, or were they merely separate "departments" of a single domain (the *respublica christiana*)? Could authorities in one domain legitimately intervene in the other? If they could, on what grounds and in what circumstances? Were either the temporal and spiritual authorities supreme, in the sense that they had legitimate jurisdiction over the other? What was the source of authority? In what ways was supreme authority limited? What gave these questions a different cast from those posed in the preceding "great debate" was that they arose not out of disputes between Church and Empire over universal jurisdiction, but rather out of conflicts between temporal and spiritual authorities within territorially limited kingdoms like France and England.

On the pro-papal or hierocratic side, these questions were addressed in part by Boniface's bulls themselves. As mentioned above, these were not particularly innovative statements of the hierocratic viewpoint—indeed, the pope himself said he considered them to be little more than proclamations of long-settled Church doctrine. What was novel was that these arguments were now being directed against kingdoms rather than the Empire. As the Church had seldom made strong pronouncements of a hierocratic nature in relation to kingdoms, this created the appearance of innovation—and certainly was interpreted as such by Philip and his supporters. But the ideas and arguments were mainly the same as had been made since the Gregorian reforms had been launched in the eleventh century.

On the dualist side, too, we see both restatements of existing dualist doctrine and doctrinal innovations that would set the stage for more far-reaching innovations during the second round of conflict between Boniface and Philip.

Consider, for example, the short untitled tract known from its *incipit* (or opening words) as *Antequam essent clerici* (Before There Were Priests), which was written some months after *Clericis laicos* was promulgated (1296), but before *Esti de statu* (1297). Traditionally assumed to have been written by, or on orders from, Philip's chancellor, Pierre Flotte, the purpose of this tract is narrow: to justify the king's practice of taxing the French clergy in times of war. It draws on a variety of political idioms and tropes (juristic and theological thought, the organological metaphor, natural law, etc.) to make the case that the French king had every right to tax the French Church.

On one reading, *Antequam essent clerici* is nothing more than a fairly straightforward rejoinder to *Clericis laicos*. Echoing arguments found in a number of authoritative sources (canon law, scripture, etc.), it asserted the French king's right to tax the French clergy through a series of declarations. The author began by pronouncing that, "before there were clerics, the king of France had custody of his kingdom, and he could make statutes to protect himself and the kingdom against the plots of his enemies...." Reflecting arguments found in the works of Hugh of St. Victor, Thomas Aquinas, and in scripture, he went on to assert that as the Church comprises both the clergy and the laity, *libertas ecclesiae* is not merely the liberty of the clergy, but of all Christians. The clergy, he then argued in familiar organological terms, is as much a part of the body politic as the laity and, as such, are obliged to pay taxes for the government and defence of the realm like all other members. And while he conceded that kings or other temporal powers had granted "liberties" (in the narrower sense of specific legal immunities from taxation) to the clergy, the authors declared that this did not diminish the temporal power's jurisdiction over the clergy or its right to rescind those immunities and tax the Church in times of necessity. Indeed, the author continued, since clerics could not take up arms in their own defence, they should at least provide the temporal authority with the resources necessary to protect them. In preventing French clerics from doing this, he concluded that the pope prevents them from exercising their natural right to self-defence.

However, a slightly deeper reading of the tract reveals an internal logic that departs considerably from the dualist orthodoxy that had long underpinned "the custom of France." Superficially, of course, the assertions made in the tract are neither new nor particularly controversial. One can find plenty of support for them in theology, canon law, and scripture. Read closely, however, they reveal an underlying political conception that is novel indeed: that the spiritual and temporal domains are not separate "societies" governed by coordinate powers, but rather separate "departments" within a single political society, both of which are subject to the jurisdiction of a single, temporal, power. This conception is on prominent display in three of the tract's most significant passages. First, it is evident where the author argues that *libertas ecclesiae* applies to the Church as *societas christiana* (the community of all Christians), not just the institutional Church. The principle of *libertas ecclesiae*, of course, was the ideological wellspring from which *Clericis laicos* flowed. Since the time of Gregory VII, that principle held that, within the broad *societas christiana*, the clergy constituted a discrete order that was independent of the laity, amongst whom were included temporal rulers, and thus not subject to lay jurisdiction or powers of taxation. In Boniface's view, Philip's attempt to tax the French Church in support of his war against England was simply an inexcusable violation of this principle. *Clericis laicos* was his effort to defend the liberty of the Church.

Given its centrality to Boniface's case, it is perhaps not surprising that the author of *Antequam essent clerici* forcefully challenged the principle of *libertas ecclesiae*. What *is* surprising, however, is the way he did it. Rather than rehearsing the arguments made against the principle during the Investiture Controversy (1075–1122), the author chose a new line of attack: he rejected the traditional definition of both *libertas* and *ecclesiae* that underpinned the entire principle. In the original doctrine, of course, the former term was construed as "liberty"—an expansive freedom of the institutional Church from direct control by the temporal authorities. However, the author of *Antequam essent clerici* redefined the term as "liberties"—a narrower term that in medieval times connoted not the broad freedom of a community or institution, but much more narrowly tailored legal privileges and immunities attached to individuals. He then argued that while French kings had sometimes allowed popes to grant specific liberties to clergymen in France, they had retained the right to nullify those liberties and tax the clergy if the "governance and defence" of the realm required it.

Similarly, the original doctrine assumed that the term *ecclesiae* referred narrowly to the clergy or the institutional Church. The author of *Antequam essent clerici* rejected this view, arguing instead that the Church was properly understood to comprise not just the clergy, but all the Christian faithful, priests and lay members alike. This second movement, in particular, was to have far-reaching implications, for the temporal-spiritual divide constituted the ultimate foundation for the Church's claim to freedom from the temporal authority. By effacing this divide, the author effectively folded both clergy and laity into a single undifferentiated body of royal subjects—or as he put it in the familiar organological language of the day, a single body politic. Having thus established that the *regnum* comprised a single political body, he was then able to establish the king's right to tax all members of that body in the interests of their common defence. The author then drove home the point by asserting that the clergy not only shared in a common obligation on the part of the "body and members" to subsidize the "head" for defence but had a special obligation under natural law to pay a fee for the defence of the realm since they were barred by canon law from raising "a shield in defence against a hostile sword."[1]

In *Antequam essent clerici*, then, we have one of the first articulations of the view that laity and clergy form a single

---

[1] *Three Royalist Tracts 1296-1302: Antequam essent clerici; Disputatio inter clerics et militem; Quaestio in utramque partem*, trans. and ed. R. W. Dyson (Bristol: Thoemmes, 1999), 5-7.

corporate entity subject to the authority of the king in temporal affairs. This view was more fully elaborated in another pro-
royal tract disseminated at the time, *Disputatio inter clericum
et militem* (Dispute between a Priest and a Knight), probably
published sometime in 1296–1297. As with *Antequam essent
clerici*, the tract has a narrow and concrete goal: to legitimize
Philip's taxation of the French Church in the eyes of informed
members of the laity within the kingdom of France.[2] However, in the course of making this case, the author of the
tract echoes and reinforces the novel arguments made in
Antequam essent clerici regarding the *regnum* as a unified
body politic in which both clergy and laity are subject to royal
taxation for governance and defence. Although there may
have been some literary connection between the two tracts,
it is more likely that both were simply specific expressions
of novel ideas that were beginning to crystallize in France in
the late twelfth century against the backdrop of rising regnal
powers and the elimination of the universal Empire as a com-
peting type of temporal authority.

    Disputatio inter clericum et militem took the form of a
dispute between a clerical advocate for Boniface's position and a knight arguing Philip's position. It opened with
the priest asserting the hierocratic position and the knight
roundly refuting it. The polemicist-knight's first rejoinder to
the priest was traditional enough. In response to the cleric's suggestion that the spiritual power was supreme in both
the spiritual and temporal domains, the knight argued that
"just as earthly princes cannot decree anything with regard
to your spirituals, over which they have not received power,
so neither can you do so with regard to their temporals, over
which you have no authority."[3] The knight then proceeded,
however, to make a genuinely innovative argument, even if
its purpose remained traditional and dualist. Simply put, the
polemicist-knight responded to the priest's assertion that the
pope is the vicar of Christ and therefore omnipotent by argu-

---

2 *Three Royalist Tracts*, trans. Dyson, xxvii.

3 *Three Royalist Tracts*, trans. Dyson, 15.

ing that "there were two times of Christ: one of humility and the other of power. That of humility was before His Passion, and that of power after His resurrection."[4] He then went on to accept that Peter was indeed appointed as Christ's vicar, but only with respect to the time of humility, not that of power and glory. Therefore, the power conferred on Peter and his successors was not that of temporal kingship (which Christ had explicitly rejected during His time of humility), but of purely spiritual lordship. In this way, the knight cleverly accepted the priest's hierocratic premise but rejected his hierocratic conclusion. Popes were supreme only concerning the spiritual domain, leaving kings supreme in respect of the temporal—the classical dualist argument at the heart of "the custom of France." Finally, the polemicist-knight attempted to counter the priest's strong suit, the *ratione peccati* argument, by claiming (somewhat unconvincingly) that if priests have jurisdiction over every matter involving sin, then they will have jurisdiction over everything and that the temporal courts might as well close down. He ended by quoting Christ in the Gospel of Luke (12:14), who, when asked to adjudicate in an inheritance dispute, declared, "Man, who made me judge or divider over you?" The author of the tract seemed to believe that Christ's denial of any judicial role in temporal matters subsequently bound his successor Peter and thus all subsequent popes.

Having more or less convincingly disposed of the priest's opening arguments in favour of papal supremacy, the polemicist-knight then turned to the task of establishing the French king's right to tax the French clergy. Kings and princes, he argued, have both a duty to defend the realm and a derivative right to raise taxes for that purpose. With respect to the taxation power, he put his case thus: "For it is granted by plain reason that the commonwealth should be defended at the commonwealth's expense and that it is entirely just that every part of it which enjoys such defence should shoulder the burden along with the others."[5] When pressed by his

---

4 *Three Royalist Tracts*, trans. Dyson, 17.

5 Dyson, *Three Royalist Tracts*, 39.

interlocutor, the polemicist-knight conceded that the temporal powers had sometimes granted privileges and immunities to certain clergy (though, emphatically, not their property). But these grants, he argued, were not irrevocable. Rather, as they were granted for the public good of the commonwealth, so they could be rescinded for the public good of the commonwealth. He concluded that not only should the clergy be grateful for the generosity of princes in making the original grant of privilege, and so happy to contribute to the princely purse when necessity appears, but they should also recognize that any such grants made by princes to the Church would be revoked if the interests of the kingdom demand it.

This is where the tract began to go far beyond the traditional dualist argument that there were two coordinate domains, the spiritual and the temporal, and that popes were supreme in the former while princes were supreme in the latter. Throughout this part of the document, the knight was at pains to establish the king's supreme authority. While recognizing the heteronomous shackles that limited the king in practice, the knight claimed that the king of France was both the supreme judge and the supreme lawmaker in his kingdom. He argued that at the time of the "fraternal division" of the Empire on the death of Louis the Pious in 840, the kingdom of France withdrew from the Empire and that "whatever authority the Empire itself formerly held in the part that was withdrawing...[was] ceded by it to the prince or king of the Franks in the same fullness."[6] The king thus recognized no superior temporal authority within his kingdom—indeed, although he did not use the precise formulation, the author was clearly invoking the doctrine of *rex in regno suo est imperator regni sui* (the king in his kingdom is the emperor of his kingdom). In short, the knight argued that there was no restriction on what the king of France could do if he thought it in the kingdom's interests. He grounded this supreme temporal authority in natural law, prescriptive right, and the historical division of Charlemagne's empire into East and West.

---

6 Dyson, *Three Royalist Tracts*, 43.

Most of this part of the tract, though, is devoted to making the case not merely that the king is supreme within his kingdom, but with effacing the line that had traditionally divided that kingdom into two discrete societies: the temporal and spiritual. As we have seen, the traditional dualist view was that the temporal and spiritual realms were distinct societies, each with their own powers and jurisdictions, and each headed by distinct authorities deriving their power directly from God. Like *Antequam* before it, *Disputatio* started out as a defence of this view. However, in the course of countering the hierocratic line, it introduced a new element that took it well beyond the settled dualism of the time. The polemicist-knight ultimately rejected the idea that kingdoms comprise two discrete societies with two different heads. Instead, he asserted, the temporal and the spiritual domains were merely departments of the same society; both were ultimately subject to the supreme authority of a single head, the king

Chapter 4

Conflict over Jurisdiction

In 1301, tensions between Philip and Boniface flared up once
again with the arrest of the bishop of Pamiers, Bernard Saisset. Boniface had sent Saisset to France to protest continuing
abuses of the Church and to urge Philip to apply the revenues
raised from taxing the Church to a crusade. But the bishop
had done more than that—he had publicly slandered the king
and, indeed, France. In response, Philip had him arrested and
charged with treason. The problem from Philip's perspective
was that, according to canon law, Saisset was under papal
jurisdiction and thus not liable to prosecution in civil court. If
Philip were to have any chance of bringing Saisset successfully to trial, he would first have to obtain from the pope a
"canonical degradation" that would remove the bishop from
his see and strip him of his clerical immunities. In pursuit of
this dispensation, the king sent a delegation to Rome to meet
with Boniface. Concerned as always with the liberties of the
Church, however, and no doubt still smarting from the humil-
iation suffered during his last dispute with Philip, Boniface
not only refused the delegation's request but demanded that
Philip release the bishop immediately. Philip agreed to this
and permitted Saisset to return to Rome unjudged, but did so
too late to prevent the publication of two papal bulls directed
against him. In the first, *Salvator mundi*, Boniface revoked
the concessions made in *Esti de statu*. In the second, *Asculta
fili*, he asserted the pope's authority to judge kings, enumerated the Church's grievances against Philip, and summoned

France's principal ecclesiastics to Rome to judge the French king and discuss means of reforming him and his kingdom.

Once again, Philip and his supporters reacted vigorously to what they perceived to be Boniface's wholly illegitimate attempt to assert papal superiority over the French king in temporal matters. In reality, of course, those parts of *Asculta fili* that touched on the distribution of power between the spiritual and temporal realms were not particularly novel. Simply put, while it asserted absolute papal authority in the spiritual realm, it proclaimed only a qualified papal authority to exercise temporal jurisdiction in cases where sin was involved (*ratione peccati*)—a doctrine first made explicit in Innocent III's decretal *Per venerabilem* and adhered to by all subsequent popes. As Boniface was later to try to explain, it did not imply papal supremacy in temporal affairs except in certain limited cases where the temporal authorities had gravely erred. However, whereas in the thirteenth century these arguments had been primarily directed against the emperor as part of the Church's long-running struggle to maintain the liberty of the Church (*libertas ecclesiae*), now they were being applied to territorial kingdoms like France—kingdoms that had hitherto enjoyed almost complete operational control of their territories and considerable jurisdiction over their regnal churches. The novelty of Boniface's confrontational approach to France, coupled with the hierocratic tone of the bull, must have left the impression that Boniface was engaged in a radically new political project—one intended to subjugate the kingdom of France to Rome. Perhaps not surprisingly, the reaction of Philip and his supporters to *Asculta fili* was ferocious indeed.

The ferocity of this reaction was on display almost immediately. When the Archdeacon of Narbonne attempted to present the bull to Phillip on February 10, 1302, a member of the king's court seized it from his hands and threw it into the fireplace. The king's supporters then set about suppressing Boniface's actual bull, preventing it from circulating to the French clergy. Having accomplished this, Philip's men—almost certainly with the king's knowledge and approval—proceeded to circulate a forged bull, known as *Deum time* (Fear God). This forgery effaced the nuanced theological arguments underpinning (and limiting) Boniface's claim to ultimate (though not operational) supremacy under the doctrine of *ratione peccati*, falsely representing Boniface as asserting that the king of France was absolutely subject to him in both spiritual and temporal matters. This forged bull was followed by a similarly forged reply, known as *Sciat maxima tua fatuitas* (May Your Very Great Fatuity Know), which further inflamed passions among those favouring the king and his cause.

Ratcheting up the pressure even more, Philip forbade the French bishops from going to Rome to attend the ecclesiastical council called by Boniface. He then summoned a council of his own to meet in Paris in April 1302. At this council, generally regarded as being the first-ever meeting of the French Estates General, Philip's chancellor delivered an impassioned speech in which he denounced Boniface for seeking to usurp not only the king's authority in temporal matters but also the ancient liberties of the French Church in matters spiritual. As intended, the speech galvanized resistance to what was portrayed as Boniface's goal of reducing the kingdom of France to a fief of the Apostolic See. In the debate that followed, the deputies from the nobility and the towns proclaimed themselves willing to sacrifice their lives in defence of the independence of France. Both estates then put their seals to letters enumerating the various charges made against Boniface, whom they referred to contemptuously as "he who at the moment occupies the seat of government of the church." For their part, the clergy adopted a less hostile tone, but essentially sided with the king, warning Boniface that his call for a council to judge Philip had placed the French Church in grave danger and imploring him to abandon the whole enterprise. The council then appointed a delegation to deliver the letters to the College of Cardinals, which it dutifully did on June 24, 1302.

The delegation was received in a public consistory at Anagni. Cardinal Matthew of Acquasparta responded to the letters first, forcefully denying the claim that the pope was attempting to usurp the French king's temporal authority. *Asculti fili*, the cardinal argued, merely reiterated established church doctrine that all men, even kings, are subject to the pope's spiritual jurisdiction and that their acts can, therefore, be judged by him on spiritual grounds. Boniface himself offered the second formal response. He began by censuring Philip's chancellor for disseminating the falsified bull *Deus time*. He then proceeded to deny the claim that he was seeking to make France a papal fief, suggesting that as a doctor of both canon and civil law, he simply could never have entertained such a ludicrous idea. Finally, Boniface emphatically stated that the ecclesiastical council he had called to judge Philip would continue as planned and instructed French clergymen to attend or face the loss of their sees.

Determined to undermine Boniface's planned council, Philip and his supporters took a number of extraordinary steps to prevent French ecclesiastics from travelling to Rome, including threatening to confiscate the property of any French churchman who attended the council. The result was predictable. When it convened on October 30, 1302, fully half of the French prelates failed to attend, and of those who did, a substantial number were sympathetic to the king and his cause. Attendance was also skewed regionally; as a result of intense lobbying on the part of Phillip's men, almost no prelates from the north of France participated. Divided internally and representative of only part of the French Church, the council was thus effectively hobbled from the outset. Doubtless to Philip's relief, it pronounced no finding or judgment relating to the king's alleged abuses of the French Church. Indeed, although the proceedings have not survived, it appears that the council achieved nothing of consequence other than condemning Philip's chancellor, Pierre Flotte.

But if the council was a setback for the pope, he quickly recovered, launching another offensive against Philip before the end of November. This time, though, the assault took the form of neither a direct attack on Philip's policies nor a specific judgment of his conduct. Instead, Boniface's assault came in the form of a bull, *Unam sanctam*, that mentioned neither Philip nor France, but that instead articulated in general terms the theological case for papal supremacy. Promulgated on November 18, 1302, the bull began by asserting the premise that the "holy, catholic, and apostolic church" is the mystical body (*corpus mysticum*) of Christ and that, as such, has only one head, Christ's vicar, the Roman pontiff. The bull then went on to state that the Roman pontiff, as head of Christ's mystical body, wielded two swords (i.e., powers): the spiritual one, which he wielded directly; and the temporal one, which is wielded by the earthly power, but under the supervision of the pontiff. Explicitly citing the hierocratic writings of Pseudo-Dionysius, the bull then made the case that the spiritual power is above the temporal "in dignity and nobility" and that by virtue of this the "spiritual power has to institute the earthly power and to judge it if it has not been good." Echoing Aquinas, the bull concluded with an emphatic statement of papal supremacy: "therefore we declare, state, define, and pronounce that it is altogether necessary for the salvation of every human creature to be subject to the Roman pontiff." Notably absent were any complicated proofs or temporizing language. Although it drew on established theological arguments regarding hierarchy (Pseudo-Dionysius), the theory of the Two Swords (Bernard of Clairvaux), and the superiority of papal jurisdiction (Hugh of St. Victor, Thomas Aquinas), and leavened these with juristic concepts regarding the mystical body of Christ, the document is less an *argument* for the hierocratic thesis than it is a bold *assertion*, grounded in precedent and tradition, of the doctrine of unqualified papal supremacy over all temporal rulers.

The French response to *Unam sanctam* was somewhat slow in coming, but it was decisive when it did. In March 1303, the Estates General met once again, this time roundly denouncing Boniface as a false pope, simoniac, thief, and heretic. In June, another meeting of the prelates and peers of the realm took place in Paris. At this meeting, supporters of Philip arranged to have twenty-nine formal charges of heresy brought against the pope. Boniface denied the charges, of course, formally clearing himself of them at a consistory at

Anagni in August 1303. He then went on the counterattack, excommunicating several prelates, suspending the university of Paris' right to confer degrees in law and theology, and reserving all vacant French benefices to the Apostolic See. Fatefully, he also prepared the bull *Super Petri solio*, which would have formally excommunicated Philip and released his subjects from their obligations to him. Before he could promulgate it as planned, however, Boniface was seized by Philip's men who planned to force him to abdicate or, failing that, bring him to trial before a general council in France. The plan quickly fell apart, however, and he was released from captivity three days later. He returned safely to Rome on September 25, only to die of a violent fever on October 12, 1303.

If the first round of conflict between Boniface and Philip opened up new lines of inquiry regarding the character, source, and locus of supreme political authority, it had done so in a necessarily halting and partial way. On the one hand, papal pronouncements were more clumsy assertions than carefully considered legal, theological, or philosophical arguments. On the other hand, *Disputatio inter clericum et militem* and *Antequam essent clerici* were little more than short tracts attempting to justify Philip's policies by applying the dualist arguments developed in connection with earlier conflicts between the Church and Empire to the conflict between the Church and the territorial kingdom of France. Although they introduced some novel arguments, they were hardly models of legal, theological, or philosophical argumentation. Partly this was a function of the relatively short duration of the conflict. The total time elapsed between the promulgation of *Clericis laicos* and that of *Esti de statu* was no more than about eighteen months. In part, however, the thinness of the arguments advanced by both camps at this time was also, at least in part, a function of the novelty of the conflict itself. Earlier in the century (indeed, going all the way back to the Investiture Controversy), the dualist–hierocratic argument had taken place in the context of two at least aspirationally "universal" political institutions, the Church and the Empire. This time, though, the underlying conflict was between the

Church and the territorially limited kingdom of France. On the pro-royal side in particular, the translation of arguments initially developed in the context of the *imperium* to the *regnum* raised thorny questions not only about the relationship of royal power to imperial power, but also about the relation of the regnal churches to the universal, and the relationship of royal to imperial jurisdiction. Addressing these questions was simply beyond the abilities of the first round of polemicists.[1]

While the complications associated with attempting to translate dualist arguments from the *imperium* to the *regnum* did not in any way disappear, during the second round of conflict both pro-royal and pro-papal thinkers were able to develop arguments that were more scholarly, more rigorous, and ultimately more innovative than those of the first round. To be sure, these thinkers were also hurried—as evidenced by the poorly edited and somewhat inelegant character of the writings they produced. However, the three most important tracts of this period were written by scholars of the highest calibre, intimately familiar with the theological, philosophical, and even juristic debates over the relationship of the spiritual power to the temporal that were regularly rehearsed at schools like the university of Paris. Unlike the polemicists who preceded them, they were very much up to the intellectual challenge of addressing the issues raised in the new conflict between *regnum* and *imperium*.

On the pro-papal side, probably the first major tract in date of composition was Giles of Rome's *De ecclesiastica potestate* (On Ecclesiastical Power). Giles, the former Prior-General of the Augustinian Friars and serving archbishop of Bourges and primate of Aquitaine, was a highly regarded scholar who enjoyed considerable influence in the papal curia. He wrote *De ecclesiastica potestate* between February and August 1302 with the express purpose of supporting Boniface in his struggle with Philip. The work itself was an

---

1 Eric Voegelin, *History of Political Ideas, Volume III: The Later Middle Ages*, ed. David Walsh, The Collected Works of Eric Voegelin 23 (Columbia: University of Missouri Press, 1998), 54.

elaborate and relentless defence of the hierocratic position, motivated in equal measure by personal loyalty to Boniface and intense commitment to the papal cause. Though it was novel in that it directed its claims of papal superiority toward kings and kingdoms rather than the emperor and the empire, it does not appear that its author intended to break any new thematic or conceptual ground. Indeed, Giles used only those sources and authorities that had been routinely pressed into hierocratic service during the previous century's conflict between the *imperium* and the *sacerdotium*. To be sure, *De ecclesiastica potestate* was unprecedented in the degree to which it pushed well-worn hierocratic arguments to their logical extremes. Ultimately, however, the tract is perhaps best understood as the apotheosis of what had, by the beginning of the thirteenth century, become an established tradition of hierocratic argumentation. Although it was not apparent to Giles and others in the pro-papal camp at the time, it was also to be the death rattle of that tradition.

Given the haste with which it was apparently written, it is perhaps not too surprising to find that *De ecclesiastica potestate* is poorly organized, repetitive, and at times even incoherent. However, a careful reading of the text reveals three significant lines of argumentation regarding the locus, source, and character of supreme authority. The first of these establishes that there are, in fact, two forms of power—the temporal power of princes (in terms borrowed from St. Bernard, the "material sword") and the spiritual power of the Church (the "spiritual sword")—and that the spiritual power precedes the temporal in time, dignity, and authority. Giles grounds this argument in Neoplatonist–naturalistic logic, Christian revelation, and history. Concerning the first of these, he began by asserting that everything in the world is naturally subject to something higher than itself. Echoing both St. Augustine and Pseudo-Dionysius, Giles put it thus:

> Therefore, if we wish to see which power stands under which power, we must attend to the government of the whole mechanism of the world. And we see in the government of the universe that the whole of corporeal substance is gov-

erned through the spiritual. Inferior bodies are indeed ruled through the superior, and the more gross through the more subtle and the less potent through the more potent; but the whole of corporeal substance is nonetheless ruled through the spiritual, and the whole of the spiritual substance by the Supreme Spirit: that is, by God.[2]

The implications of this were clear to Giles. Having demonstrated that the spiritual is superior to the corporeal or material, he then proceeded to draw the following inference regarding the relationship of the spiritual powers to the temporal:

Just as in the universe itself, the whole of corporeal substance is ruled through the spiritual...so among the faithful themselves, all temporal lords and every earthly power must be ruled and governed through the spiritual and ecclesiastical power; and especially through the Supreme Pontiff, who holds the supreme and highest rank in the Church and in Spiritual power. But the Supreme Pontiff himself must be judged only by God. For...it is he who judges all things and is judged by no one; that is, no mere man, but God alone.[3]

And then, having established the superiority of the spiritual power over the temporal, Giles proceeded to tease out the implications of this for the temporal power. If the spiritual power was supreme, he argued, then the use of both material goods and temporal powers must necessarily be ordered toward spiritual ends; otherwise, it would "lead not to salvation, but to the damnation of the soul."[4] If this were true, he continued, then it necessarily followed that temporal authority must exercise its governmental powers and material possessions to advance the purposes specified or sanctioned by the spiritual power. And if this were true, he concluded, then

---

2 R. W. Dyson, *Normative Theories of Society and Government in Five Medieval Thinkers*, 161.

3 *Giles of Rome on Ecclesiastical Power: The* De ecclesiastica potestate *of Aegidius Romanus*, trans. R. W. Dyson (Woodbridge: Boydell, 1986), 26–27, as cited in Oakley, *The Mortgage of the Past*, 197.

4 *Giles of Rome on Ecclesiastical Power*, trans. Dyson, 91.

the failure of the temporal authority to use its possessions and powers to advance those purposes was to invite legitimate censure from the spiritual power.

In a sense, Giles first established ecclesiastical supremacy by simply "reading it off" the natural hierarchic order of the universe. Not content with this naturalistic argument, however, he also attempted to establish the superiority of the spiritual power by reference to Christian revelation and theology. He began by arguing that scripture clearly revealed that priests existed before kings. Adam, Abel, and Noah were all priest-like figures (by virtue of their offering sacrifices to God) and made their appearance in salvation history long before the first king, Nimrod. He then pressed his case further, arguing that among the Jewish forebears of the Christian people, it was the priestly Moses who first delegated the adjudication of temporal disputes to a distinct temporal power. Giles concluded this line of argument by pointing out that Saul, the first actual king of the Jews, was invested by the priest Samuel. At this point, Giles appropriated and reworked an argument first made by Hugh of Saint-Victor (ca. 1098–1142) in the decades following the Investiture Controversy. Hugh had argued that while Christ's body was an organic whole comprising both the spiritual and temporal domains, the priesthood had a greater dignity than kingship because it was instituted prior in time. However, whereas Hugh was merely talking about the greater dignity needed by priests if they were to be able to consecrate kings, Giles argued that, because it was prior in time, the spiritual power was actually superior to the temporal in both dignity *and authority*. Indeed, he argued, because it was prior in time, and because it actually instituted (rather than merely consecrated) the temporal power, the spiritual power could judge the prince and, if necessary, withdraw his temporal authority. Going even further, Giles concluded that, since a "superior and primary power" can do anything that an included "inferior and secondary power" can, the spiritual power had a legitimate right to intervene in all temporal matters. Ordinarily, he conceded, the Church leaves such matters to the prince; its power in temporal matters is "superior and primary," but not usually "immediate and executory." Nevertheless, Giles insisted, the Church retained the right to exercise "occasional" jurisdiction in the temporal realm—and to do so at its own discretion.

In addition to the naturalistic and theological arguments he put forth, Giles also sought to establish the supremacy of the spiritual power by investing the Church with supreme *dominium*—that is, power over temporal things and persons. His argument in this connection was simple yet inspired. He began from the premise that true or full *dominium* must be based on justice, which he defined in Augustinian terms as "the virtue which distributes to each what is due to him."[5] True *dominium* thus required that vassals render due fealty to their lords in return for the goods and powers they held from them. Failure to render a superior due fealty necessarily resulted in the forfeiture of those goods and powers that that superior had conferred on the subordinate. Here Giles cited the example of the knight who fails to render due fealty to his lord and is therefore deprived of *dominium* over his castle. Giles then extended the argument about justice from the temporal realm to the spiritual. All owe fealty to God, he argued, but by virtue of both original and actual sin deprive Him of that fealty. As a result, God dispossesses humans of the *dominium* over property and persons that he had conditionally granted them. The Church, however, has the sacramental power to efface the stain of original sin through baptism and that of actual sin through penance. Those princes who avail themselves of the sacramental ministrations of the Church are thus able to render due fealty to God and are in turn, therefore, able to exercise legitimate *dominium* over their properties and subjects. Those who cannot or will not avail themselves of the sacraments of baptism or penance—whether unbelievers or excommunicates—are neither true kings, nor true owners of their property. In Giles' own words: "there are no true kingships among the unbelievers;

---

5 *Giles of Rome on Ecclesiastical Power*, trans. Dyson, 139.

rather, according to what Augustine says, there are only certain great bands of robbers."[6]

This line of reasoning led Giles to two conclusions regarding the locus, source, and character of supreme authority. First, it led him to conclude that supreme temporal jurisdiction over persons was vested in the Church (or, more specifically, in the papal office). The only true *dominium* was that which was subject to the Church, which itself instituted and supervised the restricted *dominium* exercised by temporal powers, and which alone could annul or extinguish it. The *dominium* of the Church was thus "superior and primary," while that of kingdoms was "inferior and secondary." Second, it led him to conclude that the Church's *dominium* concerning material goods was such that the possessions of the faithful are actually the Church's property. Giles argued that *dominium* over property, like *dominium* over persons, is derived "from the Church and through the Church." While conceding that the laity may exercise a particular and inferior "lordship of use" (*dominium utile*), he insisted that the Church retained the universal and superior right of direct ownership (*dominium directum*). Significantly, Giles also claimed that a corollary of this superior form of *dominium* was that the Church had the right to recover her property from those (ab)using it—a claim that directly contradicted then-widely circulating arguments that kingdoms were the inalienable property of kings.

Beyond establishing the supremacy of the spiritual realm, Giles also established the supremacy of the pope within both the spiritual and temporal realms. He began by defining the source and scope of the pope's power. Christ, he argued, created the papal office and, by entrusting to it the keys to the kingdom of heaven, invested it with *plenitude potestatis* or the fullness of power. Drawing on both the decretals of Innocent III and the canonist Hostiensis' standard treatment of the concept, Giles defined *plenitudo potestatis* as the power to do without a secondary cause (i.e., as the power to do directly) whatever he can do with a secondary cause (i.e., through an

---

6 *Giles of Rome on Ecclesiastical Power*, trans. Dyson, 141.

intermediary)—that is, to command, legislate, and judge in any matter whatsoever, spiritual or temporal. Because the pope enjoyed this power, he was, in effect, unrestrained by any earthly constraint or limitation—neither civil nor canon law nor precedent nor custom bound him in any way. He could suspend any law, reverse any judgment, or command on any issue. He was subject to no legal process—Church councils and temporal courts alike had no jurisdiction over him. Moreover, because the pope enjoyed the fullness of power within the Church, he could not be bound by the pronouncements of earlier popes (which, inconveniently for Giles, sometimes recognized limits on papal power). Any pope could simply set aside the judgments of his predecessors and govern as he saw fit. The pope, Giles concluded succinctly, was truly "a creature without a halter or bridle."

This fullness of power, Giles argued, operated with equal effect in both the spiritual and temporal realms. He grounded this claim in scripture, arguing that as Christ charged Peter with the duty to feed every one of His sheep (i.e., to care for all the Christian faithful, clergy, and laity alike), and as He imposed no limits on the binding and releasing power He granted to Peter (Matthew 16:18–19), papal jurisdiction must necessarily be universal—no one could be considered exempt from the pope's authority. Concerning the spiritual domain, this meant that all the power that Christ granted the Church was, in fact, vested in the pope as the embodiment of the Church. The pope was thus the font of all power within the Church; all power flowed from him like multiple streams from a single source. The authority of all priests and prelates, therefore, derived from the pope. In the temporal realm, the papal fullness of power meant that the pope was responsible for supervising, and if necessary correcting, the conduct of the inferior and secondary temporal power. No prince was exempt from papal authority, and the pope had an absolute right to intervene in any temporal matter whatsoever.

Giles conceded that "normally and ordinarily" popes refrained from directly administering the affairs of lesser powers in both the temporal and spiritual realms. In the same way that God ordinarily leaves the natural world to function according to its own laws, so too the pope ordinarily respects the jurisdiction of the temporal and spiritual princes. Giles argued that there are good reasons for this routine division of labour: to preserve as far as possible the ordinary relationship between the powers; to spare clergy from the distraction of mundane affairs; and because it would simply be impractical for the pope to administer all aspects of the day-to-day affairs of either the Church or the temporal kingdoms under his jurisdiction. However, he cautioned, this did not in any way derogate from the absolute power of the papacy. Drawing on the work of Hostiensis, he argued that there were, in fact, two forms of power through which popes govern the world: "regulated" and "absolute." Regulated power is rule-governed power. Popes normally subject themselves to the established human laws of the Church and the *regnum*, permitting their temporal and spiritual subordinates to exercise their ordinary jurisdictional power. They voluntarily refrain from randomly, capriciously, or arbitrarily disturbing the jurisdiction of temporal or security authorities. Absolute power, on the other hand, is not rule-governed. It is the pope's extraordinary power to transcend human law and jurisdiction. God and the pope alike, Giles argued, enjoy a plenitude of power. Moreover, just as this plenitude of power grants God the discretionary authority to suspend the laws of nature and to perform miracles; so, too, it grants the pope the discretionary authority to suspend the laws of man to do what is right and just.

To this point, Giles' arguments regarding absolute and regulated power were not particularly innovative. There was precedent in both the decretals of Innocent III and the writings of Hostiensis for the argument that a pope can operate outside the ordinary framework of canon and civil law "with cause" (*ex causa*). Where Giles does innovate, however, is with respect to the range of causes that would enable the exercise of this absolute power. As he put it, the pope may intervene in cases that have a spiritual dimension; that involve crime or mortal sin; where temporal conflicts threaten the peace; that involve perjury, heresy, usury, or sacrilege; when the material sword is absent and injured parties have no recourse other than to the spiritual power; where the temporal lord has permitted an appeal to the spiritual power to become customary; and in any cases that cannot be resolved by the temporal power. To Giles, then, the list of *ex causa* exceptions that enable the exercise of absolute power is all-inclusive. There was simply no limiting principle curbing the pope's power—he could, at his discretion, command, legislate, and judge in respect of any matter whatsoever, temporal or spiritual.

According to Giles, then, the power of the pope is not just supreme, but absolute. In one of the earliest and most forcefully argued cases for unfettered power concentrated in a single office, he argued that the pope is the *de iure* ruler of the entire world with ultimate jurisdiction over all people and ultimate ownership of all things. To an extent unparalleled among contemporary advocates of royal power, Giles also emphasized the role of the will of the pope and correspondingly de-emphasized the role of normative constraints like positive law, custom, and the *ius gentium*. He also effectively effaced the line separating spiritual and temporal domains. According to him, all jurisdictional power in the *societas christiana* lay ultimately with the pope—both the temporal and spiritual swords were in his hand. Even when papal claims to universal and supreme authority in matters temporal and spiritual were extinguished, these ideas continued to circulate throughout Latin Christendom in secularized form. Indeed, it is possible to draw a direct link between Giles' thought and the kind of political absolutism first expressed in the *Leviathan* of Thomas Hobbes.[7]

Giles' Augustinian colleague at the university of Paris, James of Viterbo, also argued around this time for papal supremacy but did so on grounds very different form Giles. In his 1302 tract, *De regimine christiano* (On Christian Government), James outlined what has been characterized as a Thomistic–Aristotelian version of the hierocratic perspective. He began by

---

7 Voegelin, *History of Political Ideas, Volume III*, 53.

invoking the Aristotelian premise that the political community is natural—i.e., that the fulfillment of human nature can only be achieved within governed societies. As James put it:

> The institution of communities or societies proceeded from the natural inclination itself of men, as the Philosopher [Aristotle] shows in the first book of *The Politics*. For man is by nature a social animal and living in a multitude, which results from natural necessity, in that one man cannot live in self-sufficiency on his own, but needs help from another.[8]

But whereas Aristotle had maintained that only the *polis* or city-state could be a "perfect society"—that is, an ideal self-sufficient society within which human nature could be fully realized—James, in common with most of his Aristotelian contemporaries, argued that the *regnum* or kingdom was in fact the highest form of human society, for it alone (in their eyes, at least) had the necessary scale, self-sufficiency, and orientation toward the common good to be considered "complete." He then went on to argue that the Church (in the broad sense of all the faithful) had all the defining characteristics of a *regnum*: it was a self-sufficient unity, governed by a supreme authority and ordered toward the goal of promoting a life of virtue (the good life) amongst its members. This being the case, James concluded that the Church must be considered a true *regnum*—a *regnum ecclesiae*.

Not satisfied with establishing that the Church was a *regnum ecclesiae*, James next proceeded to establish that the Church was, in fact, the only perfect *regnum*, superior in all ways to merely temporal kingdoms. Drawing on the Aristotelian principle that "that which is prior in perfection is posterior in generation and time," he first argued that households (which came into existence first) are less perfect cities (which came second); cities less perfect than kingdoms (which came next); and kingdoms less perfect than the *regnum ecclesiae* (which came last). Moreover, he argued, the *regnum ecclesiae* was the most self-sufficient, for it alone provided not only for

---

8 As quoted in Canning, *Ideas of Power in the Late Middle Ages*, 40.

physical needs but also "everything which suffices for the salvation of men and the spiritual life." The Church was also, he argued, superior to other kingdoms in that it was "holy, catholic, and apostolic" and thus ordered toward the most virtuous end or purpose. In a related vein, James drew on Augustine's interpretation of Cicero to argue that "no community is called a true *res publica*, except the ecclesiastical, because in it alone exists true justice, true utility and true communion."[9] And finally, James argued that the *regnum ecclesiae* was superior to temporal kingdoms because, whereas the latter had merely natural origins (in the Aristotelian sense), the Church had spiritual origins as well. Citing the Thomistic principle that "grace does not abolish nature, but perfects and forms it," he concluded that while temporal powers were natural and therefore legitimate, the Church had both natural *and* spiritual origins and was therefore perfect. He further concluded from this line of reasoning that the Church could both sanctify kingdoms, thereby making them more perfect (if not as perfect as the Church), and withdraw that sanctification if the lesser power fails to act correctly.

In the second part of *De regimine christiano*, James turned his attention from ecclesiology toward what was clearly the prime motivating question behind this work: what was the locus, source, and character of "the power of Christ the king and His vicar"? To answer this question, he first established that power comes in three forms: the power to work miracles, the power to pray and to administer the sacraments (sacramental power), and the power of jurisdiction (royal power). James himself set aside the power to work miracles as not being germane to his purpose, and for the purposes of this study, we can further set aside his discussion of sacramental power as being similarly immaterial. How, then, did James conceive of the pope's royal power—that is, his power to judge. He began by exploring the nature of royal power *qua* royal power. It was, he concluded, essentially a coercive power, wielded by a public authority and directed toward the

---

9 Canning, *Ideas of Power in the Late Middle Ages*, 46.

common good. Its efficient cause or source was God. James then argued that this inherently governmental power came in two distinct forms: royal power over temporal matters (*potestas regia temporalis*) and royal power over spiritual matters (*potestas regia spiritualis*). The former, he argued, was the power usually wielded by kings governing the *regnum*'s temporal affairs; the latter, the power wielded by clergy to judge in matters of sin. To be sure, James argued, these two forms of royal power differed in terms of their "mode of action": "the one determines spiritual causes, the other temporal; the one imposes temporal or corporal penalties, the other spiritual...The temporal feeds in a bodily fashion and the spiritual in a spiritual...."[10] However, he insisted, they were substantially similar in kind or nature.

James thus established that both priests and princes wielded jurisdictional power—they both possessed the royal power to judge, even if they judged in respect of different matters. Having done so, he then set about exploring the differences between these two forms of power. This he did primarily in terms of their respective purposes and jurisdictions. The temporal power (or, as James sometimes refers to it, the "secular power") was by its very nature ordered to the earthly goods necessary for men to lead lives of virtue. Its purpose was the regulation of the things of this world rather than the next. It had jurisdiction only over the laity, and then only in connection with the administration of temporal affairs. In Aristotelian terms, the temporal power had to do with nature. The spiritual power, on the other hand, was by nature ordered toward the spiritual goods necessary for eternal salvation. Its purpose was the regulation of heavenly things, rather than earthly. The spiritual power had jurisdiction over clergy and laity alike. It was primarily concerned with grace and the supernatural, rather than with power and the natural.[11]

---

10 James of Viterbo, *De regimine Christiano: A Critical Edition and Translation*, ed. and trans. R. W. Dyson (Leiden: Brill, 2009), 207.

11 James of Viterbo, *De regimine Christiano*, ed. Dyson, 209.

Perhaps predictably, James concluded that of these two forms of royal power, *potestas regia spiritualis* was superior.[12] While he conceded that the temporal power was prior in time, he insisted that spiritual power was superior concerning *dignity* and *causality*. The spiritual power, James asserted, was "simply and absolutely" superior in dignity because the spiritual is ordered toward a higher end than the temporal, and because the object of temporal power is man as a natural being, that is, "man as perfectible by grace."[13] The spiritual power, he argued, was superior with respect to *causality* in that the "temporal power exists for the end of the spiritual," and "the higher is that to the end of which the end of the other is ordered."[14] Moreover, while conceding that the temporal power arises out of men's natural inclinations, he argued that this power remains imperfect and unformed unless perfected and formed by grace. As it was the spiritual power that conferred this perfecting and forming grace on the temporal, the former was necessarily superior to the latter. Finally, James argued that the spiritual power, having perfected the temporal power through grace, could withdraw that grace if it judged that the temporal power had acted "unworthily."[15] As it is in the nature of things that superiors judge inferiors (and not the reverse), this proved that the spiritual power was superior to the temporal.

Having established the superiority of the royal or jurisdictional power possessed by clergy, James demonstrated that the pope's royal power is superior to that possessed by all other priests and prelates. The Church, he argued, is organized as a hierarchy in which priests are inferior to bishops, bishops to archbishops, and so on. As in all hierarchies, in this hierarchy there must be one who is primary and supreme—that is, one who holds the spiritual power "in the highest

12 James of Viterbo, *De regimine Christiano*, ed. Dyson, 207.

13 James of Viterbo, *De regimine Christiano*, ed. Dyson, 209.

14 James of Viterbo, *De regimine Christiano*, ed. Dyson, 209–11.

15 James of Viterbo, *De regimine Christiano*, ed. Dyson, 215.

degree and principally and according to fullness" and who is the source of all such power.[16] In the Church, this primary and supreme power was Christ. However, James argued that because Christ's "bodily presence was withdrawn from the Church, it was fitting that the entire government of the Church should be committed to someone who should rule the Church in His place and on His behalf."[17] This person was Peter, upon whom Christ conferred the fullness of power (*plenitudo potestatis*) necessary for the salvation of men. All spiritual power within the Church was subsequently derived from him and all members of the clergy subject to his jurisdiction. The pope was the supreme judge in spiritual matters, his rulings subject to no appeal because there were none superior to him to whom an appeal might be made. For similar reasons, a pope could not be judged. Christ further willed, James asserted, that this fullness of power might be passed on to Peter's successors so that there would always be a single, omnipotent "Vicar of Christ" mediating between Christ and His Church.

Drawing the threads of his argument together, James concluded that the pope had superior jurisdiction not only over all spiritual affairs but over all temporal ones as well. He exercised his *plenitudo potestatis* over all members of the church militant—secular princes no less than clerical ones. Temporal rulers derived their royal power from the pope and only possessed this power in diminished and derivative form. The pope had the right to intervene in any temporal matter, *ratione peccati*. No member of the Church (in the broad sense of the community of all the faithful) was exempt from his jurisdiction, and all were obliged to obey his commands—even if they contradicted those of the temporal power. The pope possessed the power to judge all and impose spiritual and temporal penalties whenever he considered it necessary for the salvation of the faithful. James conceded that there was still an important role to be played by the temporal power. Ordinarily, popes would leave the administration of tempo-

---

16 James of Viterbo, *De regimine Christiano*, ed. Dyson, 173.

17 James of Viterbo, *De regimine Christiano*, ed. Dyson, 173.

ral affairs to the immediate agency of the temporal power, both out of respect for the hierarchy of powers and to free the clergy to attend to spiritual matters. In other words, he accepted that there were two swords, the material and the spiritual, and that they were ordinarily wielded by the temporal and spiritual powers, respectively. Ultimately, though, he argued that both swords belong to the pope, one (the spiritual) to use and the other (the material) to command. Indeed, it is possible to read James as arguing that the two powers are not really two powers at all, but only two parts of the same unified power in possession of the "king of kings" (the pope).

On the pro-royal side, an anonymous dualist tract *Quaestio in utramque partem* (Both Sides of the Question) was published sometime between December 1301 and September 1303. The primary purpose of this tract was to offer a classic defence of the dualist thesis, adapted to the new circumstances of papal–regnal (as opposed to papal–imperial) conflict. It considered the relationship between papal authority on the one hand and imperial and royal authority on the other, posing and then answering two fundamental questions: were the spiritual and temporal domains separate and distinct? And, did the pope possess supreme authority in both domains? Although it adopted a balanced approach and a measured tone, the tract nevertheless came down decisively on the royalist side. Drawing on a range of philosophical, theological, canonical, and civil law sources, the author unambiguously concluded the pope had temporal jurisdiction over neither secular princes in general nor the king of France in particular.

While the document rehearses many of the standard dualist arguments, and while some of its attempts at innovation fall short of the mark, *Quaestio in utramque partem* makes two significant contributions to the evolving discourse regarding the locus, source, and character of supreme authority. First, the author of the tract introduced the argument that spiritual and temporal matters differ in kind—i.e., they are of different *genera*, corresponding to the dual nature of human beings—and that, therefore, royal and papal jurisdictions also differ in kind. The hierocratic perspective, of course, assumed a Pseudo-Dionysian hierarchy of difference in which the powers were similar in kind, united in the person of one supreme authority who then delegated power to his temporal and spiritual subordinates. On this monist view, because the spiritual power has greater dignity than temporal power, and because greater things contain within themselves lesser things, those who have power in spiritual things also have it in temporal things. The author of *Quaestio in utramque partem*, in contrast, explicitly rejected the Pseudo-Dionysian hierarchy of difference, arguing that as the two powers had different objects, they were simply different classes or types of power. Therefore, the relationship between them was not one of hierarchical dependence, but of horizontal and reciprocal *inter*dependence. In the words of the tract's author, "there is a mutual dependence, because the temporal needs the spiritual because of the soul, whereas the spiritual needs the temporal on account of its use of temporal things."[18] The pope was thus deemed supreme in the spiritual domain and the secular princes supreme in their respective temporal domains. Significantly, the author of *Quaestio in utramque partem* also concluded that the pope's *plenitudo potestatis* was operative only in the spiritual domain. In the temporal domain, the prince's power was derived directly from Christ, unmediated by the pope.

However, if, on the whole, the *Quaestio in utramque partem* deepened and strengthened the dualist argument, it simultaneously undermined it in significant ways. Most obviously, it weakened the idea that Christian society comprised two discrete domains by recognizing that the pope had jurisdiction over temporal matters when those matters were, in the words of Pope Innocent III's decretal *Novit*, "mixed with sin." While the tract's author was careful to limit this jurisdiction, drawing on canon law to conclude the king of France may be subject to the pope only "incidentally and in special circumstances,"[19] the net effect was to leave intact

---

18 Canning, *Ideas of Power in the Late Middle Ages*, 26.

19 *Three Royalist Tracts*, trans. Dyson, 81.

the *ratione peccati* bridge linking the pope's spiritual power to the king's temporal affairs. More significantly, however, and cutting in a different direction, the *Quaestio in utramque partem* both rehearsed established arguments for French independence from, and equality with, the Empire and introduced some novel ones. As we have seen with other political thinkers of the time, the very effort to establish French independence from papal jurisdiction based on the French king's supreme authority within his realm necessarily resulted in and required further elaboration of French claims to independence from the Empire. In *Quaestio in utramque partem*, two new types of argument were advanced in support of France's *de iure* independence. On the one hand, the author argued from history that, as France had emerged before the Empire, and since that time had enjoyed an *imperium* (i.e., supreme and unlimited authority) that had never been extinguished by the Empire or any other power, it was an independent kingdom. On the other hand, the author argued from law that, even if that *imperium* had been extinguished by conquest, France had now enjoyed *de facto* independence from the Empire for at least a century. Under the terms of canon law, the author continued, this meant that France enjoyed *de iure* independence by virtue of customary right. In turn, this meant that the French king now enjoyed within his kingdom the *imperium* that the emperor enjoyed within his (now territorially limited) empire. In translating the dualist argument from the context of papal–imperial conflict to one of papal–regnal conflict, the author of *Quaestio in utramque partem* had thus revived and rejuvenated ideas regarding the locus of supreme authority that had first emerged almost a century earlier. These ideas were to become one of the keystones of the emerging regnalist thesis—a thesis that would ultimately displace the dualism that *Quaestio in utramque partem* had set out to defend.

Another anonymous pro-royal tract, formally called *Quaestio de potestate papae* (The Question of Papal Power), but more commonly known by its incipit, *Rex pacificus* (The Peacemaker King), was published sometime early in 1302. Like the

Quaestio in utramque partem, this tract set out to translate classical dualist argument from the context of papal–imperial conflict to one of papal-regnal conflict. And, as with the *Quaestio*, in so doing it developed a line of argumentation that ultimately went far beyond the logic of dualism. Indeed, through its reworking of well-worn concepts and the introduction of new ideas, the tract so thoroughly contradicted the logic of dualism that it can be read as a precursor of the starkly regnalist views developed by Marsilius of Padua two decades or so later.

Rex pacificus was organized into four discrete parts. The first and fourth parts enumerated and then refuted the pro-papalist arguments. In the second part, the author presented the arguments in favour of the supremacy of the temporal power. The third part drew on a range of scriptural, patristic, juristic, philosophical, and theological sources to make the case that while the Church may have had moral authority, only the king exercised true jurisdiction or political power. The first, second, and fourth parts were not particularly original, though they were indeed notable for their methodical, concise, and clear presentation. The third part, though, truly *was* innovative, introducing arguments regarding the locus, source, and character of supreme authority that Ullman said have "more in common with French political thought of later centuries than with the views current at the beginning of the fourteenth century."[20]

The author of *Rex pacificus* began the third part of the tract with a relatively straightforward dualist argument, though he presented it through a somewhat novel allegorical fashion. Man, he asserted, is a microcosm of the universe composed of two elements or substances—the corporeal or earthly and the spiritual or angelic. The corporeal element refers to man's physical substance, "the body and its members"; the spiritual to his mind or soul, comprising the powers

---

20 Walter Ullmann, "A Medieval Document on Papal Theories of Government," *The English Historical Review* 61, no. 260 (1946): 180–201, at 201.

of "memory, intellect, and will."[21] These two dimensions of man he allegorized as the "head" (the seat of the soul/mind) and the "heart" (the fountainhead of life-giving blood). The author then argued that, just as individual humans have this dual nature, so does society. At the social level, the function of the head is performed by the spiritual power, the function of the heart, by the temporal power. Moreover, he concluded that "just as in the human body the workings of the heart and head are distinct, so also are the jurisdictions involved in worldly government distinct."[22] Circling back to this point much later in the text, the author made clear that this meant that "both the spiritual jurisdiction, which the pope has, and the temporal jurisdiction, which the king has in his kingdom, are entirely distinct and separate, so that just as it is not the king's place to interfere in matters of spiritual jurisdiction...so the pope ought not to interfere in matters of temporal jurisdiction...."[23] Part three of the tract thus opens with a powerful restatement of the classical dualist thesis that earthly government involves the governance of two distinct domains ruled by two coordinate powers that do not meddle in each other's affairs.

As the author of *Rex pacificus* proceeded to enumerate the defining characteristics of the two powers, however, his argument began to take on a decidedly more regnalist hue. The head, he proceeded to elucidate, as the seat of the mind, has available the faculties of discernment and wisdom. It uses these faculties to decide between morally good and bad actions. The head then, via the "nerves" that connect it to the members, rules or directs the body to act accordingly. At the social level, the author continued, the pope performs the functions of the head, for it is he who possesses the faculties of moral discernment and wisdom necessary to direct men to the good and away from the bad (i.e., toward salvation and away from damnation). As with the human body, the pope directs the mystical body (the Church in the broad sense)

---

21 *Three Royalist Tracts*, trans. Dyson, 75.

22 *Three Royalist Tracts*, trans. Dyson, 75.

23 *Three Royalist Tracts*, trans. Dyson, 99.

through a kind of "nervous system": the subordinate offices and ranks of the clergy (the Church in the narrow sense). The function of these intermediary ecclesiastical powers is to convey the moral prescriptions, exhortations, and example of the pope to the faithful. Although he does not say it explicitly, throughout this passage, the author strongly intimates that the pope can be said to have only persuasive or hortatory powers over the Christian faithful. At no point does he assign the papal office any coercive powers to command, legislate, or judge in the temporal domain.

Analogously, the author of *Rex pacificus* discussed the defining characteristics of the temporal power. The heart, he asserted, is the foundation of the body; it is the wellspring of the life-giving blood that the arteries carry throughout the body. Similarly, he analogized, the king is the source of life-giving laws and justice that his officials carry throughout the commonwealth. Furthermore, just as human life cannot be sustained without blood, so political life cannot be sustained without just and enforceable laws. Citing Jerome's commentary on Jeremiah, he concluded that this meant that the function of kings is "to give judgment, do justice, and to deliver the oppressed from the hand of those who persecute them."[24] By its very nature, then, kingship entails the possession and use of coercive power to make and enforce just laws. Compared to the merely persuasive power (which is not really power at all) wielded by the pope, this monopoly of coercive power unambiguously establishes that the king is the sole locus of supreme authority in the temporal realm. This is a far cry from the dualist thesis the author initially set out to defend.

To adapt the dualist argument to the context within which he is writing, the author of *Rex pacificus* employed an analogy that, when fully developed, ended up draining the spiritual authority of any real power, and vesting all true (i.e., coercive) power in the king. But the mutation of dualism into regnalism did not stop there. Next, the author attempted to ground the separation of temporal and spiritual powers

---

24 *Three Royalist Tracts*, trans. Dyson, 77.

in scripture and authoritative scriptural commentary. In the Old Testament, he began, God decreed that the Jewish people should be guided by both temporal and spiritual leaders—that is by chieftains, judges, and kings on the one hand, and by priests and prophets on the other. By divine ordinance, the two powers were kept apart; they are always referred to in scripture as separate. Neither is recorded as having meddled in the affairs of the other, except on those rare occasions when priests exercised temporal power with the authorization of the temporal power. Thus, the author concludes that popes may exercise some limited degree of temporal power, but only with the prince's permission. Otherwise, the two powers should refrain from interfering in each other's domains.

Thus far, the author's argument from scripture had an unambiguously dualist tone. At this point, however, he sounded several decidedly more regnalist notes. First, he cited St. Isidore of Seville as proof that temporal powers have ultimate authority over the Church. Isidore's dictum was that princes have a God-given duty to protect the Church and be held accountable by God for how well they discharge that duty. On the basis of this assertion, the author of *Rex pacificus* concluded that "...concerning temporal things, the Church is given over, and made subject, to the power of kings and princes."[25] He then argued that while the Old Testament was devoid of even a single reference to a priest giving commands to a king, it is replete with references to situations in which kings gave commands to priests and prophets. Finally, the author of the tract argued that three of the most noteworthy kings in the Old Testament—David, Hezekiah, and Josiah—routinely gave commands to priests, and the priests obeyed. From this, he concluded that Old Testament kings were "lords next after God in authority, over whom neither prophets nor priests claimed any kind of authority which might diminish their temporal lordship."[26] Applying this insight to his own

25 *Three Royalist Tracts*, trans. Dyson, 82.
26 *Three Royalist Tracts*, trans. Dyson, 83.

time, he then drew the explicitly dualist conclusion that, the pope is not the supreme authority in temporal affairs.

Not satisfied with simply invoking the kings of the Old Testament to make his case, the author of *Rex pacificus* next proceeded to justify the superior jurisdiction of the temporal power by appealing to Christ's example and teachings. He pointed out, for example, that when asked to divide an inheritance, Christ declined in such a way as to convey that jurisdiction with respect to hereditary property did not belong to Him. The author then argued that, as the disciple cannot be above the master, if Christ (the master) denied Himself temporal jurisdiction over property, it was surely denied to the pope (the disciple). No less authority than St. Bernard was then invoked to drive home the point. Bernard was quoted as stating that the apostles never sat in judgment of boundary disputes and property claims. Their power, he said, lay in forgiving sins, not in dividing property. For them to sit in judgment over such matters, he asserted, would be "to invade the territory of another" (the temporal power). The author of *Rex pacificus* then developed a parallel line of reasoning: Christ Himself had abjured temporal jurisdiction when He said, "My kingdom is not of this world." The author, drawing on the writings of John Chrysostom, interpreted this utterance as definitively establishing that Christ sought no temporal power or jurisdiction. As Christ's vicar cannot logically claim powers exceeding those claimed by Christ, the author logically concluded that Christ did not intend to transfer authority over temporal kingdoms to the pope.

In his Old and New Testament proofs, the author of *Rex pacificus* set out to defend the traditional dualist thesis that the pope exercised no jurisdiction over kings' temporal goods. But the substance and tone of the arguments he advanced ultimately went far beyond his self-professed goal of defending dualism. Put simply, by the time he had finished defending the dualist thesis, the author had made the case that only kings had true, supreme power in the temporal realm; and that popes not only had no such power but that they were subject to the king's authority and jurisdiction. To be sure, nothing in the tract even hinted that kings had authority over the Church with respect to preaching, doctrine, or the sacraments. That would have been impossible within the dualist thought-world of that era. However, the author of the tract did make clear that kings had jurisdiction over the temporal goods of the Church and that clergy were subject to the jurisdiction of lay courts with respect to temporal matters. Whatever his avowed objectives, this was a long way from the dualist thesis or the "custom of France."

Arguably the most important pro-royal tract produced during the second round of conflict between Philip and Boniface was the *De potestate regia et papali*, written and revised several times by John of Paris (Jean Quidort) between mid-1302 and early 1303. John, a highly regarded member of the faculty at the university of Paris, was a supporter of the French crown—a fact attested to by his decision to join his fellow Dominicans in signing the June 1303 petition calling for the pope to be tried before a general council of the Church. Despite his pro-regnal proclivities, however, he did not write *De potestate regia et papali* as a polemical tract dealing specifically with the conflict between Philip and Boniface. Instead, he wrote it as a scholastic work meant to examine the generic or philosophical relationship between the *regnum* and the *sacerdotium*. As a result, the tract has the structure and tone of a calm, relatively dispassionate, and scholarly treatment of the issues in question. It relentlessly marshals scriptural, canonistic, patristic, Aristotelian–Thomistic, and contemporary polemical sources to challenge the hierocratic thesis. Although formally structured as a blow-by-blow refutation of the main philosophical arguments of hierocrats like Giles of Rome and James of Viterbo, John's treatise also made a positive case for the supremacy of kings.

In some ways, *De potestate regia et papali* mounted a fairly typical defence of the dualist thesis; its arguments were similar to the anti-hierocratic arguments developed over the preceding century or so, differing from them mainly in that, as with *Quaestio in utramque partem* and *Rex pacificus*, it focused on the question of papal power over the *regnum* rather than the *imperium*. The treatise began in a fairly conventional manner, defining both the temporal power (kingship) and the spiritual power (priesthood). With respect to kingship, John developed an essentially Aristotelian argument that political society is natural in the sense that man is, by nature, a social and political animal. Humans need to live in communities, he continued, because they cannot supply themselves with all the necessities of life (food, clothing, protection) required for the "good life" and because they have the capacity for speech, the natural purpose of which is to communicate with others. Ideally, he continued, men would live in "perfect communities"—that is, communities of sufficient scale to provide all of life's necessities and thereby establish the conditions within which its citizens could pursue lives of virtue. John then drew the essentially Thomistic conclusion that, as they lacked sufficient scale to provide these necessities, neither the household nor the village could be considered a "perfect community." Nor, however, could a universal empire, which by its very nature was of a scale that rendered it ungovernable. Only the kingdom, he concluded, had the scale necessary to provide the food, clothing, and protection "for a man's whole life"; only the kingdom could be considered a perfect community.[27] Having established the kingdom as the perfect community, John then argued that such communities required governance to assure that they were ordered correctly toward the common good. Departing from Aristotle, who ultimately preferred a mixed constitution, John insisted that the best form of governance for the perfect community of the kingdom was "kingship"—that is, "rule over a community perfectly ordered by one person to the common good."

Shifting his attention to the priesthood, John then argued that humans are not solely ordered toward the kind of good that can be acquired through nature—the Aristotelian good

---

27 From John of Paris, *Tractatus de potestate regia et papali*, in *Quaestio de potestate papae (Rex pacificus). An Enquiry into the Power of the Pope: A Critical Edition and Translation*, ed. and trans. R. W. Dyson (Lewiston: Mellen, 1999), 8.

life—but also have a supernatural end, eternal life. However, this supernatural end cannot be realized solely through human virtue; it requires grace or divine virtue. When Christ walked the earth, He was the source and dispenser of this grace and thus the supreme authority concerning supernatural ends. In preparation for his eventual Ascension, however, Christ instituted ministers or priests who would act in his stead, dispensing the grace necessary for eternal life through the sacraments. The sole function of ministers or priests, John therefore concluded, was to exercise "the spiritual power given by Christ...for dispensing the sacraments to the faithful."[28] John's priesthood was thus understood to be an entirely spiritual institution, different in kind from kingship.

Having established that the two powers were separate domains, John then examined the nature of hierarchy within each. The spiritual sphere, he argued, is subject to divine law and is thus organized according to the logic of the celestial hierarchy. Therefore, it is necessarily a graded order comprising—in ascending order of "superiority and completeness of power"—priests, bishops, the pope, and God. In this hierarchy, authority flows in descending fashion from God to the pope, from the pope to the bishops, and from the bishops to the priests. John was at pains to emphasize that the Church is thus an ordered unity—a single, universal institution governed by a single supreme authority, the pope, and ordered toward the end of promoting eternal salvation. In the temporal realm, however, John came to a radically different conclusion. Here, he argued, the governing law was not divine, but natural. The celestial hierarchy's logic did not apply; neither, therefore, did the Pseudo-Dionysian principle of unity. Men are naturally inclined not only to form political societies, John wrote, but also to choose different rulers and systems of rule according to their particular needs and circumstances. There is nothing in natural law that compels all men to live under a single supreme temporal power. Indeed, he quoted Aristotle to the effect that the existence of multiple and diverse polit-

---

28 John of Paris, *Tractatus de potestate regia et papali*, ed. Dyson, xxv.

ical societies was natural and, therefore, desirable while a universal empire governed by one man was not.

Having compared the differing natures of hierarchy in the *regnum* and *sacerdotium*, John next compared them in terms of priority in time, dignity, and causality (power). Concerning time, he argued that, if priesthood were understood to include the anticipatory or figurative priests of the Old Testament, then kingship and priesthood emerged simultaneously. If, however, one accepted that there were no true priests before Christ, then kingship was prior in time to the priesthood by at least two millennia. He draws no explicitly political conclusions from this, but the argument clearly strikes a blow at hierocratic claims that priests are prior in time. Turning next to the question of dignity, John conceded that priesthood, because it pertained to man's supernatural ends, was, in fact, prior to kingship. However, he quickly moved on to deny that this priority in dignity implied that the temporal power derived in any way from the spiritual or that the latter enjoyed superior jurisdiction. Both powers, he insisted, derived their authority directly from a single superior power, God, and neither was therefore generally or absolutely subordinate to the other. The superior divine power granted each power the supreme authority in its respective domain. In this way, John maintained the important Pseudo-Dionysian principle of unity, but displaced the locus of that unity from the pope upward to God. In the process, he drained the principle of its political force by establishing that the temporal and spiritual domains enjoyed hierarchical equality rather than a sub- and super-ordination relationship.

John's final task was mostly to tease out the implications of the hierarchical equality of the two powers (regnal and ecclesiastical). His method of argument was to examine, first, papal dominion over property and, second, papal jurisdiction over people. With respect to dominion, which he defined as the possession of property rights, John first argued that the pope had no dominion over the Church's material goods. This is so, he reasoned, because ecclesiastical goods had originally been donated to the Church as a corporate whole, rather than to any individual cleric, and were therefore owned by the Church as a corporate whole, not by any individual cleric. Clergymen merely exercise stewardship over these goods, using them to advance the spiritual goals of the Church. The pope, therefore, does not exercise lordship over ecclesiastical goods. He is merely the "administrator," "manager," or "steward" of those goods. John further argued that the pope exercises neither dominion nor stewardship over the goods of the laity. Lay property, he reasoned, was not originally donated to the community as a whole as was Church property. Instead, individual laypeople acquired their property through their own art, labour, and industry. Having acquired property in this way, laypeople were thus vested with the natural right to use, administer, hold, or alienate it as they saw fit—neither prince nor pope had any claim to lay property, except perhaps in cases of dire emergency. John drove the point home by pointing out that, as Christ Himself had not claimed dominion over the laity's material goods, He could hardly transfer it to His successors.

Drawing a clear distinction with dominion, John defined jurisdiction as the legitimate authority to govern and rule. He then argued that there was no scriptural warrant for the hierocratic claim that Christ had vested in the papacy with such authority in both the spiritual and temporal domains. Rather, he argued, Christ instituted two discrete powers and vested each of those powers with only those elements of His supreme authority to rule relevant to their respective ends or purposes. Kings were thus vested with the authority to rule their kingdoms, popes with the authority to rule the Church. John qualified this somewhat by arguing that each of the two authorities possessed "conditional and accidental" power over the other. The Church had the power to punish and coerce incorrigibly sinful princes; the temporal power, the authority to depose incorrigibly errant popes. But he carefully limited these indirect or incidental powers and, in the papal case, explicitly conditioned the pope's right to act against a wayward prince on the approval of the prince's temporal subordinates. In classical dualist fashion, John was careful to preserve the distinctiveness and hierarchical equality of the two ruling authorities.

Finally, John addressed the key question of whether the Donation of Constantine had conferred papal jurisdiction over the kingdom of France. He concluded that it did not. First, John argued, the Donation affected only a limited portion of the Empire, Italy. France was not included in the grant. Second, the Donation was invalid. Here John cited Accursius' "Great Gloss" on the Civil Law to the effect that the emperor was not authorized to diminish and despoil the Empire by alienating its western half. Third, even granting the validity of the Donation, it was never within the competence of a Roman emperor to donate the Frankish lands to anyone since they were not his to donate. John supported this claim by arguing that while the earlier inhabitants of France, the Gauls, may have been subject to the Romans, the later inhabitants, the Franks, never were. Never having been subjugated by Rome, France could not, therefore, be alienated by it. Fourth, even if the Donation were valid, and further conceding that the original donation had lawfully included France, the pope would still have no temporal dominion or jurisdiction over the French king because the Donation would have been abolished by customary right. France had ruled itself as an independent kingdom for over a century, John argued, and customary law dictated that after such a lengthy period of self-rule, dominion and jurisdiction must be considered transferred from the pope to the king of France. He concluded his argument by citing scripture and scriptural commentary to the effect that, as the Roman Empire had been founded on force, its jurisdiction could be similarly thrown off by force.

In writing *De potestate regia et papali*, John had provided Philip and his supporters with a powerful dualist rejoinder to the increasingly strident hierocratic claims of Giles of Rome, James of Viterbo, and Henry of Cremona. In the course of mounting this defence of the dualist thesis, however, he made several assumptions, assertions, and arguments that were ultimately more regnalist than dualist in nature. This was perhaps most evident in connection with his treatment of the locus of supreme authority to command, legislate, and judge. In this connection, John's most significant innovation was to naturalize the *regnum* as the locus of supreme authority. Like James of Viterbo, John grounded his entire argument on the Aristotelian premise that both society and government were natural. But whereas James had insisted that the temporal power must be sanctified by the spiritual if it were to be truly just and perfect, John insisted that "the Regnum, as the highest form of natural society, can be fully perfect in a strictly natural sense without the necessity of sanctification by the Church."[29] However, if the *regnum* was the highest form of natural society, it was always only potentially so. To ensure that it remained ordered toward the common good, understood in terms of the Aristotelian-Thomistic idea of the good life, each *regnum* required a governor—that is, a single person, a king, charged with steering the kingdom in the right direction. Moreover, if these kings were to carry out their essential functions, they required certain powers. These powers were those of temporal jurisdiction—the powers to command, legislate, and judge in temporal affairs. John concluded that the source of all these powers was God and that kings, therefore, were subject to no higher power save God Himself.

But what, specifically, was the *character* of this supreme authority to rule or govern. For John, the answer to that question was to be found in the concept of "jurisdiction." John began his examination of jurisdiction by first differentiating it from dominion, with which it had often been confused or conflated. Jurisdiction, he argued, was the power to govern or rule through the law, while dominion referred to possession of property rights. Having thus disentangled these two phenomena, John then set about specifying jurisdiction's various entailments. Jurisdiction *qua* jurisdiction, he argued, was always the same phenomenon: whether wielded by the temporal or spiritual power, it always referred to the power to govern or rule in the interests of the common good. To the extent

---

29 John B. Morrall, *Political Thought in Medieval Times*, 2nd ed. (London: Hutchinson, 1960), 90.

that the jurisdiction of kings differed from that of popes, it did so not in terms of the nature of the power itself, but rather in terms of the object of that power. Popes had supreme jurisdiction over the institutional Church—that is, they had the power to command the clergy and to determine what was just and unjust in disputes among the clergy. They also exercised stewardship over the Church's corporately owned property. Popes did not, however, exercise either dominion or jurisdiction over the goods of the laity. Nor did they exercise any jurisdiction in the temporal affairs of the *regnum*. Nor, finally, did they possess any coercive power to enforce their will beyond the institutional Church. Kingdoms were simply not the proper object of papal jurisdiction. On the other hand, John argued, kings did possess supreme jurisdiction over the kingdom. They could command their subjects and make and enforce laws. And, unlike the popes, kings had the power to punish and coerce wrongdoers—indeed, although he does not say it explicitly, John clearly implied that kings enjoyed an ultimate monopoly of legitimate coercive power within their respective kingdoms.

Significantly, John saw this supreme temporal jurisdiction not only as natural, but as a positive good. Within the previously regnant Augustinian tradition, governance and kingship had been understood as an unfortunate, if necessary, byproduct of original sin.[30] As Augustine himself had argued, pre-lapsarian humans were by nature *social* animals, but not *political* ones; before the Fall, people socialized naturally and had no need for coercive institutions that impinged on human liberty. After humanity's Fall, however, coercive power and authority became necessary as both a punishment and remedy for sin. Kingship, therefore, was a necessary evil. Within the Aristotelian tradition John drew on, however, human beings were understood to be "political animals" whose very nature—even before the Fall—required them to live within a *political* community (*polis*). For thinkers like John, the politi-

---

30 For a discussion of Augustinian views of the state see Canning, *A History of Medieval Political Thought*, 40–43.

cal community was necessary and good because only within such a community was the cultivation of virtue (toward which humanity was naturally inclined) fully possible.[31] Similarly, governance and authority were also good for, without them, the community could not be steered toward its appointed end. On this view, supreme political authority—provided it was exercised in the common good, and not for private benefit—was seen as a positive good rather than a necessary evil.

Although John argued that the king held *supreme* temporal jurisdiction, he did not claim that it was *absolute*. John understood supreme authority to be limited primarily by the principle of what has subsequently been called "popular consent." He argued that each kingdom was a *universitas* ("corporation") and that each king, as head of his *universitas*, derived his regal powers from the body of the *universitas*. Initially developed in classical times to refer to "associations of persons in both public and private law,"[32] by the twelfth century, jurists had taken up the concept to define the structure of small groups within the Church (a cathedral chapter, for example) as well as the universal Church itself. By the end of the thirteenth century, jurists had begun to apply the logic of corporation theory to kingdoms as well. In both cases, they defined the corporation as a community: possessing a distinctive legal personality; shaped by its own unique customs, purpose and composition; and simultaneously "composed of a plurality of human beings and an abstract unitary entity perceptible only to the intellect."[33] The jurists also fashioned a doctrine of the proper relationship between the corporation, its members, and its "head." Basically, the head of the corporation was the embodiment of the legal person of the corporation and enjoyed considerable authority to act autonomously on its behalf. Significantly, however, corporation theory also

---

31 John Finnis, *Aquinas: Moral, Political, and Legal Theory* (Oxford: Oxford University Press, 1998), 114.

32 Pennington, "Law, Legislative Authority, and Theories of Government," 443.

33 Canning, *A History of Medieval Political Thought*, 172.

placed strict limits on this authority. Above all, the head of the corporation was required to honour the customs and constitution of the corporation, to seek the counsel and consent of its members, and to act in its best interests. Breach of this contract between the head of a corporation and its members constituted grounds for the removal of the head.[34] Supreme jurisdiction then, John implied, was not without "halter and bridle" as Giles of Rome had claimed in connection with the pope. The nature of the royal office, divine law, the *ius gentium*, customary law, and even the "constitution" of the realm all imposed constraints on kings—constraints that were ultimately enforceable by "the people electing" (the barons and peers) taking steps to depose the king, either on their own initiative or at the instigation of the pope.

---

34 For a discussion of corporation theory see Pennington, "Law, Legislative Authority, and Theories of Government," 444–49; and Brian Tierney, *Religion, Law, and the Growth of Constitutional Thought*, 19–25.

Epilogue

At the time of Boniface's death in 1303, there were two basic constellations of ideas regarding the locus, nature, and character of supreme authority in circulation throughout Latin Christendom. On the one hand, polemicists and scholars had revived the traditional hierocratic perspective, adapting arguments first made in connection with the papal–imperial conflicts of the early thirteenth century to the quite different conditions of royal–papal conflict at the turn of the fourteenth century. For them, supreme authority was unambiguously vested in the pope or the papal office—the supreme pontiff possessed a *plenitudo potestatis* over all members of the church militant—secular princes no less than clerical ones. Temporal rulers derived their royal power from the pope and possessed this power only in diminished and derivative form from him. The pope had the right to intervene in any temporal matter, on account of sin (*ratione peccati*). Popes ultimately possessed two forms of power: "regulated" or rule-governed power, and "absolute" power, defined as the pope's extraordinary power to transcend human law and jurisdiction. In increasingly strident terms, hierocratic polemicists and scholars made the case that the pope was truly "a creature without a halter or bridle."

On the other hand, pro-royal thinkers had adapted the older imperial–dualist arguments of the early thirteenth century to the ongoing dispute between Phillip and Boniface. In this case, though, it was not merely a matter of dusting off old arguments and expressing them more forcefully and uncompromisingly than in the past. Rather, in translating the dualist argument from the context of imperial–papal conflict to one of regnal–papal conflict, pro-royal polemicists and scholars developed a radically new paradigm of supreme temporal power. In this new regnalist paradigm, kings (rather than emperors) ruled territorially limited kingdoms (rather than a universal empire); the authority to rule in the temporal sphere came directly from God, without papal mediation or sanctification; and the Church was understood to be less a distinct society subject to its own laws and exercising unqualified dominion over its own property, than a subordinate spiritual "department" contained within—and subject to the political jurisdiction of—the *regnum*. Moreover, in this new regnalist paradigm, the *respublica Christiana* was not seen as a single political space governed cooperatively by the temporal power (the Empire) and the spiritual power (the Church). Instead, it was understood to be a single spiritual space (the Church, in the sense of all the catholic faithful) naturally organized into territorially discrete kingdoms, all of which possessed supreme political authority internally, and none of which recognized any superior political authority externally.

Although there were some underlying social, political, and cultural dynamics that may have favoured the regnalist perspective in the long run, both the hierocratic and regnalist perspectives were viable political projects in the early fourteenth century. Both paradigms were coherent and persuasive, and both had adherents in powerful positions in both the temporal and spiritual domains. At the height of the conflict between Philip and Boniface, it simply was not clear which way the historical winds were blowing. At least dimly aware of the historical stakes, proponents of each paradigm were thus driven to make increasingly strident claims in favour of the pope or the king. With the promulgation of *Unam sanctam* in 1302, this dynamic reached its climax. Which side would emerge victorious on the intellectual field of battle? What vision would dominate the political imagination of Latin Christendom in the decades (perhaps centuries) to come?

As is often the case, these questions would be answered, not as a result of developments on the battlefield of ideas, but of those in the political arena. Sensing that he had gained the upper hand on Boniface's death, Philip demanded of the new pope Benedict XI, and Benedict's successor, Clement V, a formal condemnation of his one-time adversary. Benedict put up something of a fight, even excommunicating Philip's minister Nogaret, but died in 1304. However, his successor, Clement, faced with renewed and mounting pressure from Philip, decided that the best course of action for the papacy would be for him to try to placate the French king. To this end, he promptly rescinded the bull *Clericis laicos*. Then, in 1306 he issued a decretal, *Meruit*, that effectively annulled *Unam sanctam*. Clement subsequently suppressed the Knights Templar at Philip's behest, acquiesced in the French king's demand that Boniface be tried posthumously, and even went so far as to nullify all papal acts detrimental to the French king enacted since 1302. Finally, Clement moved the papal court to Avignon, where it increasingly fell under the French crown's influence.

By the time Boniface's trial concluded in 1311, it was evident to all that the king was triumphant, the papacy defeated, and papal claims to temporal authority over the French king effectively extinguished. It was also obvious that the regnalist thesis had emerged from the dispute as the dominant way of thinking about the locus, source, and character of supreme authority in temporal matters. Henceforth, sovereignty was understood to derive ultimately from God, though in practice from the people; the character of sovereignty was defined and delimited by concepts such as *pro ratione voluntas*, *plenitudo potestatis*, and *potesta absoluta*; and the supreme authority to command, legislate, and judge was vested in the office of the king, not the emperor or pope. While hierocratic and even imperialist–dualist ideas remained in circulation throughout the later Middle Ages, they were largely exercises in what Francis Oakley has dubbed the "politics of nostalgia."[1]

---

[1] Oakley, *The Watershed of Modern Politics*, 14–50.

They were not the ideas most characteristic of the era. Nor, significantly, were they the ones that proved the most influential when thinkers such as Bodin and Hobbes were "inventing" sovereignty in the early modern period.

Further Reading

The following is an annotated selection of books I consider to be essential reading on the topic of medieval sovereignty. I selected these books to represent a range of academic disciplines and perspectives. While far from exhaustive, this selection should satisfy those seeking a deeper understanding of the evolution of medieval European political thought and the medieval idea of sovereignty in particular.

Armitage, David. *Foundations of Modern International Thought*. Cambridge: Cambridge University Press. 2013.

> Combines indispensable methodological essays which consider the genealogy of globalization and the parallel histories of empires and sovereign states, with fresh considerations of leading modern figures such as Hobbes, Locke, Burke, and Bentham in the history of international thought.

Bain, William. *Political Theology of International Order*. Oxford: Oxford University Press, 2020.

> Makes two key contributions to scholarship on international order. First, it provides a thorough intellectual history of medieval and early modern traditions of thought and the way in which they shape modern thinking about international order. It explores the ideas of Augustine, Thomas Aquinas, William of Ockham, Martin Luther, and other theologians to rise above the sharp differentiation of medieval and modern that underpins most international thought. Second, it shows how theological ideas continue to shape modern theories of international order by structuring the questions theorists ask as well as the answer they provide.

Bartelson, Jens. *A Genealogy of Sovereignty*. Cambridge: Cambridge University Press, 1995.

> A critical analysis and conceptual history of sovereignty focused on philosophical and political texts during the Renaissance, the Classical Age, and Modernity. Notably neglects to address the medieval era.

Bisson, Thomas. *The Crisis of the Twelfth Century: Power, Lordship, and the Origins of European Government*. Princeton: Princeton University Press, 2015.

> Traces the origins of European government and the idea of sovereignty to a crisis of feudal lordship and its resolution during the twelfth century.

Black, Antony. *Political Thought in Europe, 1250–1450*. Cambridge: Cambridge University Press, 1992.

> Explores ideas of the state, law, rulership, representation of the community, and the right to self-administration, and how, during a crucial period, these became embedded in people's self-awareness, and articulated and justified by theorists. A concise overview, using the analytical tools of scholars such as Pocock and Skinner, of both medieval history and political thought. Contains a full bibliography to assist those wishing to pursue the subject in greater depth.

Cambridge History of Medieval Political Thought. Edited by J. H. Burns. Cambridge: Cambridge University Press, 1988.

> This volume, reprinted in paperback in 2010, offers a comprehensive overview of the history of the complex body of political ideas that evolved over more than a thousand years. While the primary emphasis of the volume is necessarily upon those ideas that developed within Latin Christendom, due attention is also paid to the impact of Byzantine, Jewish, and Islamic thought.

Canning, Joseph. *A History of Medieval Political Thought, 300–1450*. New York: Routledge, 1996.

> An accessible introduction to medieval political thought. Synthesizes the latest scholarship on medieval political thought, including scholarship that was previously unavailable in English. Provides the historical and intellectual context within which medieval political ideas emerged and evolved.

Coleman, Janet. *A History of Political Thought: From the Middle Ages to the Renaissance* Malden: Blackwell, 2000.

> Focuses on medieval and Renaissance thinkers, tracing the evolution of medieval political thought and its eventual evolution into early-modern political thought.

Dyson, R. W. *Normative Theories of Society and Government in Five Medieval Thinkers: St. Augustine, John of Salisbury, Giles of Rome, St. Thomas Aquinas, and Marsilius of Padua.* Lewiston: Mellen, 2003.

> A detailed scholarly examination of five major medieval thinkers who sought to bring out the political implications of the doctrines, social imaginary, and vocabulary of Christianity, as well as the role of the institutional Church in political affairs. Examines the development of the "ideology" of the medieval Church with reference to the "Gelasian principle"; Pope Gregory VII's contribution to debates regarding temporal and spiritual rule; and the decisive conflict between Pope Boniface VIII and King Philip IV of France.

Grimm, Dieter. *Sovereignty: The Origin and Future of a Political and Legal Concept.* Translated by Belinda Cooper. New York: Columbia University Press, 2015.

> An accessible introduction to the concept of sovereignty. Connects the evolution of the idea to crucial world-historical developments, from the religious conflicts of sixteenth-century Europe to the contemporary phenomenon of globalization.

Jackson, Robert. *Sovereignty: Evolution of an Idea.* Cambridge: Polity, 2007.

> This highly accessible book provides a concise and comprehensive introduction to the history and meaning of sovereignty. It covers topics such as the discourse of sovereignty, the global expansion of sovereignty, the rise of popular sovereignty, globalization and sovereignty, and the relationship between sovereignty and human rights.

Jones, Chris, ed. *John of Paris: Beyond Royal and Papal Power.* Turnhout: Brepols, 2015.

> Offers the first collection of essays in any language to be dedicated to an exploration of John of Paris's thought. Re-examines his view of the relationship between Church and state, and his conception of political organization. Breaks new ground concerning the relationship between John's various writings, the origins and development of his thought, and its political legacy.

Nederman, Cary, *Lineages of European Political Thought: Explorations along the Medieval/Modern Divide from John of Salisbury to Hegel*. Washington, DC: Catholic University of America Press, 2009.

> Examines some of the more significant historiographical and conceptual issues shaping contemporary scholarly debates regarding the medieval roots of modern political concepts.

Oakley, Francis. *The Mortgage of the Past: Reshaping the Ancient Political Inheritance (1050–1300)*. New Haven: Yale University Press, 2012.

> A magisterial three-part history of the emergence of Western political thought during the Middle Ages. Explores kingship from the tenth century to the beginning of the fourteenth, demonstrating how religious and cultural change transformed kingship into an increasingly secular political institution.

Osiander, Andreas. *Before the State: Systemic Political Change in the West from the Greeks to the French Revolution*. Oxford: Oxford University Press, 2007.

> Refutes the idea, current in International Relations theory (in particular Realism), that the fundamental nature of "international" politics is historically immutable and that the sovereign state is a transhistorical phenomenon that has existed up and down the ages.

Pennington, Kenneth. *The Prince and the Law, 1200–1600: Sovereignty and Rights in the Western Legal Tradition*. Berkeley: University of California Press, 1993.

> Investigates legal interpretations of the prince's power from the twelfth to the seventeenth century, focusing on a fascinating paradox: that the theory of individual rights co-evolved with the contradictory concept of the prince's "absolute power."

Philpott, Daniel. *Revolutions in Sovereignty: How Ideas Shaped Modern International Relations*. Princeton: Princeton University Press, 2001.

Argues that two historical revolutions in ideas are responsible for the emergence of the modern system of sovereign states: the Protestant Reformation, which ended medieval Christendom and contributed to the triumph of the sovereign state in Europe; and ideas of equality and colonial nationalism, which transformed a world dominated by European colonial empires into one defined by sovereign states.

Teschke, Benno. *The Myth of 1648: Class, Geopolitics, and the Making of Modern International Relations*. London: Verso, 2003.

> Rejects a commonplace of European history: that the Peace of Westphalia closed the Thirty Years' War and inaugurated a new international order driven by the interaction of sovereign territorial states. Concludes that 1648 is really a false caesura in the history of world order and that the real medieval-to-modern Great Divide did not open up until relatively recent times with the development of modern states and true capitalism.

Tierney, Brian. *Religion, Law, and the Growth of Constitutional Thought, 1150-1650*. Cambridge: Cambridge University Press, 1982.

> Traces the interplay between theories of spiritual and temporal of government from the twelfth century to the seventeenth. Demonstrates how ideas recovered from antiquity—Roman law, Aristotelian political philosophy, teachings of the Church Fathers—interacted with the material realities of medieval society to produce distinctively new doctrines of constitutional government.

Voegelin, Eric. *History of Political Ideas, Volume III: The Later Middle Ages*. Edited by David Walsh. The Collected Works of Eric Voegelin 23. Columbia: University of Missouri Press, 1998.

> Traces the historical roots of the modern world in medieval civilization. William of Ockham, Dante, Giles of Rome, and Marsilius of Padua all emerge in this study as providing essential precursors to modern political concepts.

Wilks, Michael. *The Problem of Sovereignty in the Later Middle Ages: The Papal Monarchy with Augustinus Triumphus and the Publicists*. Cambridge: Cambridge University Press, 1963.

> Demonstrates how during the later medieval era, theologians and literary writers, especially Augustinus Triumphus of Ancona, built up a complete theory of papal sovereignty.